Favorite Brand Name™
Dump Recipes

Publications International, Ltd.

Pictured on the front cover *(left to right):* Middle Eastern Chicken Soup *(page 18),* Peach Strawberry Cake *(page 216)* and Skillet Pasta Roma *(page 112).*

Pictured on the back cover *(left to right):* New Orleans Fish Soup *(page 48),* Blackberry Almond Cake *(page 242)* and Easy Italian Chicken *(page 176).*

ISBN: 978-1-68022-007-0

Library of Congress Control Number: 2015930185

Manufactured in China.

8 7 6 5 4 3 2 1

Microwave Cooking: Microwave ovens vary in wattage. Use the cooking times as guidelines and check for doneness before adding more time.

Preparation/Cooking Times: Preparation times are based on the approximate amount of time required to assemble the recipe before cooking, baking, chilling or serving. These times include preparation steps such as measuring, chopping and mixing. The fact that some preparations and cooking can be done simultaneously is taken into account. Preparation of optional ingredients and serving suggestions is not included.

Publications International, Ltd.

CONTENTS

SUPER SPEEDY CHICKEN   4

ONE-POT BEEF & PORK   28

SEAFOOD IN A SNAP   42

NO-FUSS VEGETABLES   52

QUICK & CREAMY   74

HEARTY BEANS   84

SUPER SPEEDY
CHICKEN

QUICK HOT AND SOUR CHICKEN SOUP

- 2 cups water
- 2 cups chicken broth
- 1 package (about 10 ounces) refrigerated fully cooked chicken breast strips, cut into pieces
- 1 package (about 7 ounces) chicken-flavored rice and vermicelli mix
- 1 jalapeño pepper,* minced
- 2 green onions, chopped
- 1 tablespoon soy sauce
- 1 tablespoon lime juice
- 1 tablespoon minced fresh cilantro

Jalapeño peppers can sting and irritate the skin, so wear rubber gloves when handling peppers and do not touch your eyes.

1. Combine water, broth, chicken, rice mix, jalapeño, green onions and soy sauce in large saucepan; bring to a boil over high heat. Reduce heat to low; cover and simmer 20 minutes or until rice is tender, stirring occasionally.

2. Stir in lime juice; sprinkle with cilantro.

Makes 4 servings

CREAMY TUSCAN BEAN & CHICKEN SOUP

    2 cans (10¾ ounces **each**) CAMPBELL'S® Condensed
       Cream of Celery Soup (Regular **or** 98% Fat Free)

    2 cups water

    1 can (about 15 ounces) white kidney beans (cannellini),
       rinsed and drained

    1 can (about 14½ ounces) diced tomatoes, undrained

    2 cups shredded **or** diced cooked chicken

    ¼ cup bacon bits

    3 ounces fresh baby spinach leaves (about 3 cups)

       Olive oil

       Grated Parmesan cheese

1. Heat the soup, water, beans, tomatoes, chicken and bacon in a 3-quart saucepan over medium-high heat to a boil.

2. Stir in the spinach. Cook for 5 minutes or until the spinach is wilted. Serve the soup with a drizzle of oil and sprinkle with the cheese.

Makes 4 servings

KITCHEN TIP: For the shredded chicken, purchase a rotisserie chicken. Remove the skin and bones. You can either shred the chicken with your fingers or use 2 forks.

PREP TIME: 10 minutes
COOK TIME: 10 minutes
TOTAL TIME: 20 minutes

CHICKEN TORTELLINI SOUP

6 cups chicken broth

1 package (9 ounces) refrigerated cheese and spinach tortellini

1 package (about 6 ounces) refrigerated fully cooked chicken breast strips, cut into bite-size pieces

2 cups baby spinach

4 to 6 tablespoons grated Parmesan cheese

1 tablespoon chopped fresh chives *or* 2 tablespoons sliced green onion

1. Bring broth to a boil in large saucepan over high heat. Add tortellini; cook over medium heat 5 minutes.

2. Stir in chicken and spinach; cook over low heat 3 minutes or until chicken is heated through.

3. Sprinkle with Parmesan cheese and chives.

Makes 4 servings

Spicy Thai Coconut Soup

3 cups coarsely shredded cooked chicken
    (about 12 ounces)

2 cups chicken broth

1 can (15 ounces) straw mushrooms, drained

1 can (about 14 ounces) light coconut milk

1 can (about 8 ounces) baby corn, drained

1 tablespoon minced fresh ginger

½ to 1 teaspoon red curry paste

2 tablespoons lime juice

¼ cup chopped fresh cilantro

1. Combine chicken, broth, mushrooms, coconut milk, corn, ginger and red curry paste in large saucepan; bring to a simmer over medium heat. Cook until heated through.

2. Stir in lime juice; sprinkle with cilantro.

Makes 4 servings

NOTE: Red curry paste can be found in jars in the Asian aisle of large grocery stores. Spice levels can vary between brands. Start with ½ teaspoon, then add more as desired.

Easy Chicken, Spinach and Wild Rice Soup

1 can (about 14 ounces) reduced-sodium chicken broth

1¾ cups chopped carrots

2 cans (10¾ ounces each) reduced-sodium condensed cream of chicken soup, undiluted

2 cups cooked wild rice

1 teaspoon dried thyme

¼ teaspoon dried sage

¼ teaspoon black pepper

2 cups coarsely chopped baby spinach

1½ cups chopped cooked chicken*

½ cup milk

*Half of a rotisserie chicken will yield about 1½ cups of cooked meat.

1. Bring broth to a boil in large saucepan over medium-high heat. Add carrots; cook 10 minutes.

2. Add soup, rice, thyme, sage and pepper to saucepan; bring to a boil. Stir in spinach, chicken and milk; cook and stir 2 minutes or until heated through.

Makes 6 servings

COUNTRY CHICKEN SOUP

5¼ cups SWANSON® Chicken Broth (Regular, Natural Goodness® **or** Certified Organic)

⅛ teaspoon poultry seasoning

⅛ teaspoon dried thyme leaves, crushed

1 medium carrot, sliced (about ½ cup)

1 stalk celery, sliced (about ½ cup)

1 small onion, finely chopped (about ¼ cup)

½ cup **uncooked** regular long-grain white rice

2 cans (4.5 ounces **each**) SWANSON® Premium White Chunk Chicken Breast in Water, drained

1. Heat the broth, poultry seasoning, thyme, carrot, celery and onion in a 3-quart saucepan over medium-high heat to a boil. Stir in the rice. Reduce the heat to low.

2. Cover the saucepan and cook for 20 minutes or until the rice is done.

3. Stir the chicken in the saucepan and heat through.

Makes 4 servings

PREP TIME: 10 minutes
COOK TIME: 30 minutes
TOTAL TIME: 40 minutes

CREAMY CHICKEN AND VEGGIE SOUP

2¾ cups chicken broth

2 cans (10¾ ounces each) condensed cream of chicken soup, undiluted

3 medium Yukon Gold potatoes, diced

1 cup finely chopped green onions, divided

2 cups diced cooked chicken

1 package (10 ounces) frozen peas and carrots

¼ cup half-and-half or whole milk

1. Combine broth, soup, potatoes and ½ cup green onions in large saucepan; bring to a boil over high heat. Reduce heat to low; cover and simmer 15 minutes or until potatoes are tender.

2. Stir in chicken, peas and carrots and half-and-half; cook until heated through. Sprinkle with remaining ½ cup green onions.

Makes 6 servings

Middle Eastern Chicken Soup

2½ cups water

1 can (about 14 ounces) reduced-sodium chicken broth

1 can (about 15 ounces) chickpeas, rinsed and drained

1 cup chopped cooked chicken

1 small onion, chopped

1 carrot, chopped

1 clove garlic, minced

1 teaspoon dried oregano

1 teaspoon ground cumin

½ (10-ounce) package fresh spinach, stemmed and coarsely chopped

⅛ teaspoon black pepper

1. Combine water, broth, chickpeas, chicken, onion, carrot, garlic, oregano and cumin in large saucepan; bring to a boil over high heat. Reduce heat to medium-low; cover and simmer 15 minutes.

2. Stir in spinach and pepper; simmer, uncovered, 2 minutes or until spinach is wilted.

Makes 4 servings

Asian Chicken Noodle Soup

3½ cups SWANSON® Chicken Broth (Regular, Natural Goodness® **or** Certified Organic)

1 teaspoon soy sauce

1 teaspoon ground ginger

Generous dash ground black pepper

1 medium carrot, diagonally sliced

1 stalk celery, diagonally sliced

½ red pepper, cut into 2-inch-long strips

2 green onions, diagonally sliced

1 clove garlic, minced

½ cup broken-up **uncooked** curly Asian noodles

1 cup shredded cooked chicken

1. Heat the broth, soy sauce, ginger, black pepper, carrot, celery, red pepper, green onions and garlic in a 2-quart saucepan over medium-high heat to a boil.

2. Stir the noodles and chicken in the saucepan. Reduce the heat to medium and cook for 10 minutes or until the noodles are done.

Makes 4 servings

KITCHEN TIP: For an interesting twist, use **1 cup** sliced bok choy for the celery and **2 ounces uncooked** cellophane noodles for the curly Asian noodles. Reduce the cook time to 5 minutes.

PREP TIME: 5 minutes
COOK TIME: 20 minutes
TOTAL TIME: 25 minutes

Chunky Chicken Soup

  1 tablespoon olive oil

  1 onion, chopped

  1 can (about 14 ounces) diced tomatoes

  1 cup chicken broth

  1 cup thinly sliced carrots

  ¼ teaspoon salt

  ⅛ teaspoon black pepper

  3 cups sliced kale or baby spinach

  1 cup diced cooked chicken breast

1. Heat oil in large saucepan over medium-high heat. Add onion; cook and stir about 5 minutes or until golden brown. Stir in tomatoes, broth, carrots, salt and pepper; bring to a boil. Reduce heat to medium-low; simmer about 10 minutes or until carrots are tender.

2. Stir in kale and chicken; cook until kale is wilted.

Makes 2 servings

Hearty Chicken Vegetable Soup

3 cans (14 ounces **each**) SWANSON® Natural Goodness® Chicken Broth (5¼ cups)

½ teaspoon dried thyme leaves, crushed

¼ teaspoon garlic powder **or** 2 cloves garlic, minced

2 cups frozen whole kernel corn

1 package (about 10 ounces) frozen cut green beans

1 cup cut-up canned tomatoes

1 stalk celery, chopped

2 cups cubed cooked chicken **or** turkey

1. Heat the broth, thyme, garlic, corn, beans, tomatoes and celery in saucepan over medium-high heat a boil. Reduce the heat to low. Cover and cook for 5 minutes or until the vegetables are tender.

2. Stir the chicken in the saucepan and heat through.

Makes 6 servings

PREP AND COOK TIME: **25 minutes**

THAI NOODLE SOUP

     2 cans (about 14 ounces each) chicken broth

    12 ounces chicken tenders, cut into ½-inch pieces

     1 package (3 ounces) ramen noodles, any flavor,
          broken into pieces*

    ¼ cup shredded carrots

    ¼ cup frozen snow peas

     2 tablespoons thinly sliced green onion

    ½ teaspoon minced fresh garlic

    ¼ teaspoon ground ginger

     3 tablespoons chopped fresh cilantro

    ½ lime, cut into 4 wedges

Discard seasoning packet.

1. Combine broth, chicken and noodles in large saucepan; bring to a boil over medium heat. Cook 2 minutes.

2. Add carrots, snow peas, green onion, garlic and ginger. Reduce heat to low; simmer 3 minutes or until noodles are tender.

3. Sprinkle with cilantro; serve with lime wedges.

Makes 4 servings

ONE-POT
BEEF & PORK

QUICK AND ZESTY VEGETABLE SOUP

1 pound lean ground beef

½ cup chopped onion

Salt and pepper

2 cans (14.5 ounces each) DEL MONTE® Italian Recipe Stewed Tomatoes

2 cans (14 ounces each) beef broth

1 can (14.5 ounces) DEL MONTE® Mixed Vegetables

½ cup uncooked medium egg noodles

½ teaspoon dried oregano

1. Brown meat with onion in large saucepan. Cook until onion is tender; drain. Season to taste with salt and pepper.

2. Stir in remaining ingredients. Bring to boil; reduce heat.

3. Cover and simmer 15 minutes or until noodles are tender.

Makes 8 servings

PREP TIME: 5 minutes
COOK TIME: 15 minutes

Kielbasa & Cabbage Soup

1 pound Polish kielbasa, cut into ½-inch cubes

1 package (16 ounces) coleslaw mix (shredded green cabbage and carrots)

3 cans (14½ ounces each) beef broth

1 can (12 ounces) beer or nonalcoholic malt beverage

1 cup water

½ teaspoon caraway seeds

2 cups FRENCH'S® French Fried Onions, divided

Garnish: fresh dill sprigs (optional)

1. Coat 5-quart pot or Dutch oven with nonstick cooking spray. Cook kielbasa over medium-high heat about 5 minutes or until browned. Add coleslaw mix; sauté until tender.

2. Add broth, beer, water, caraway seeds and *1 cup* French Fried Onions; bring to a boil over medium-high heat. Reduce heat to low. Simmer, uncovered, 10 minutes to blend flavors. Spoon soup into serving bowls; top with remaining onions. Garnish with fresh dill, if desired.

Makes 8 servings

PREP TIME: 10 minutes
COOK TIME: 20 minutes

Quick and Easy Meatball Soup

   2 cans (about 14 ounces each) Italian-style stewed tomatoes

   2 cans (about 14 ounces each) beef broth

   1 can (about 14 ounces) mixed vegetables

   ½ cup uncooked rotini pasta or small macaroni

   ½ teaspoon dried oregano

   1 package (15 to 18 ounces) frozen Italian sausage meatballs without sauce, thawed according to package directions

1. Combine tomatoes, broth, mixed vegetables, pasta and oregano in large saucepan.

2. Stir in meatballs; bring to a boil over medium-high heat. Reduce heat to medium-low; cover and simmer 15 minutes or until pasta is tender.

Makes 4 to 6 servings

Mediterranean Bean and Sausage Soup

- ½ pound sweet Italian pork sausage, casings removed
- 1 large onion, chopped
- ½ teaspoon garlic powder **or** 4 cloves garlic, minced
- 2 cups PREGO® Traditional Italian Sauce **or** Tomato, Basil & Garlic Italian Sauce
- 1¾ cups SWANSON® Chicken Broth (Regular, Natural Goodness® **or** Certified Organic)
- 1 can (about 15 ounces) black beans **or** pinto beans
- 1 can (about 15 ounces) white kidney beans (cannellini), drained
- 1 can (about 15 ounces) red kidney beans, drained

1. Cook the sausage, onion and garlic powder in saucepan over medium-high heat until sausage is browned, stirring to separate the meat. Pour off any fat.

2. Add Italian sauce and broth and heat to a boil. Reduce the heat to low and cook for 10 minutes. Add the beans and heat through.

Makes 4 servings

PREP TIME: 10 minutes
COOK TIME: 25 minutes
TOTAL TIME: 35 minutes

Lentil Soup with Ham

3½ cups reduced-sodium chicken broth

1 pound ham slice or ham steak, trimmed and cut into bite-size pieces

1 cup dried brown lentils, rinsed and sorted

1 medium carrot, peeled and diced

½ medium onion, chopped

1 jalapeño pepper,* seeded and finely chopped

½ teaspoon dried thyme

Jalapeño peppers can sting and irritate the skin; wear rubber gloves when handling peppers and do not touch your eyes. Wash hands after handling.

1. Combine broth, ham, lentils, carrot, onion, jalapeño and thyme in large saucepan; bring to a boil over high heat. Reduce heat to low; cover and simmer 30 minutes or until lentils are tender.

2. Let stand, covered, about 15 minutes before serving.

Makes 4 servings

COUNTRY JAPANESE NOODLE SOUP

1 can (14.5 ounces) DEL MONTE® Original Recipe Stewed Tomatoes

1 can (14 ounces) reduced sodium chicken broth

3 ounces uncooked linguine

2 teaspoons reduced-sodium soy sauce

1 to 1½ teaspoons minced gingerroot *or* ¼ teaspoon ground ginger

¼ pound sirloin steak, cut crosswise into thin strips

5 green onions, cut into thin 1-inch slivers

4 ounces firm tofu, cut into small cubes

1. Combine tomatoes, broth, pasta, soy sauce and ginger with 1¾ cups water in large saucepan; bring to boil.

2. Cook, uncovered, over medium-high heat 5 minutes.

3. Add meat, green onions and tofu; cook 4 minutes or until pasta is tender. Season to taste with pepper and additional soy sauce, if desired.

Makes 4 servings (1¼ cups each)

PREP TIME: 10 minutes
COOK TIME: 15 minutes

Pizza Meatball
and Noodle Soup

  1 can (about 14 ounces) beef broth

  ½ cup chopped onion

  ½ cup chopped carrot

  2 ounces uncooked whole wheat spaghetti, broken
     into 2- to 3-inch pieces

  1 cup zucchini slices, cut in half

  8 ounces frozen fully cooked Italian-style meatballs,
     thawed

  1 can (8 ounces) tomato sauce

  ½ cup (2 ounces) shredded mozzarella cheese

1. Combine broth, onion, carrot and pasta in large saucepan; bring to a boil over medium-high heat. Reduce heat to low; cover and simmer 3 minutes.

2. Add zucchini, meatballs and tomato sauce; return to a boil. Reduce heat to low; cover and simmer 8 minutes or until pasta is tender and meatballs are heated through, stirring occasionally.

3. Sprinkle with mozzarella.

Makes 4 servings

Sweet Potato and Ham Soup

1 tablespoon butter

1 leek, sliced

1 clove garlic, minced

4 cups reduced-sodium chicken broth

2 sweet potatoes, peeled and cut into ¾-inch pieces

8 ounces ham, cut into ½-inch pieces

½ teaspoon dried thyme

2 ounces stemmed spinach, coarsely chopped

1. Melt butter in large saucepan over medium heat. Add leek and garlic; cook and stir until tender.

2. Add broth, sweet potatoes, ham and thyme; bring to a boil over high heat. Reduce heat to low; simmer 10 minutes or until sweet potatoes are tender.

3. Stir in spinach; simmer 2 minutes or until wilted. Serve immediately.

Makes 6 servings

SEAFOOD
IN A SNAP

ITALIAN FISH SOUP

   1 cup meatless pasta sauce

   ¾ cup water

   ¾ cup reduced-sodium chicken broth

   1 teaspoon dried Italian seasoning

   ¾ cup uncooked small pasta shells

   1½ cups frozen vegetable blend, such as broccoli,
       carrots and water chestnuts or broccoli, carrots
       and cauliflower

   4 ounces fresh halibut or haddock steak, 1 inch thick,
      skinned and cut into 1-inch pieces

1. Combine pasta sauce, water, broth and Italian seasoning
in medium saucepan; bring to a boil over high heat. Stir in
pasta; return to a boil. Reduce heat to medium-low; cover
and simmer 5 minutes.

2. Stir in frozen vegetables and fish; return to a boil. Cover
and simmer over medium-low heat 4 to 5 minutes or until
pasta is tender and fish flakes easily when tested with fork.

Makes 2 servings

Savory Seafood Soup

2½ cups water or chicken broth

1½ cups dry white wine

1 onion, chopped

½ red bell pepper, chopped

½ green bell pepper, chopped

1 clove garlic, minced

½ pound halibut, cut into 1-inch pieces

½ pound sea scallops, cut into halves

1 teaspoon dried thyme

Juice of ½ lime

Dash hot pepper sauce

Salt and black pepper

1. Combine water, wine, onion, bell peppers and garlic in large saucepan; bring to a boil over high heat. Reduce heat to medium-low; cover and simmer 15 minutes or until bell peppers are tender, stirring occasionally.

2. Add fish, scallops and thyme; cook 2 minutes or until fish and scallops turn opaque.

3. Stir in lime juice and hot pepper sauce; season with salt and black pepper.

Makes 4 servings

Tip: If halibut is not available, substitute cod, ocean perch or haddock.

MARYLAND-STYLE CRAB SOUP

3½ cups SWANSON® Beef Broth (Regular, 50% Less Sodium **or** Certified Organic)

1 cup CAMPBELL'S® Tomato Juice

1 tablespoon seafood seasoning

2½ cups frozen mixed vegetables

1 can (about 14½ ounces) diced tomatoes, undrained

1 medium potato, cut into ½-inch cubes (about 1 cup)

1 small onion, chopped (about ½ cup)

1 container (8 ounces) refrigerated pasteurized claw **or** lump crabmeat

Oyster crackers

1. Heat the broth, tomato juice, seasoning, mixed vegetables, tomatoes, potato and onion in a 4-quart saucepan over high heat to a boil. Reduce the heat to low. Cover and cook for 1 hour.

2. Stir in the crabmeat. Cook for 15 minutes. Serve with the crackers.

Makes 6 servings

PREP TIME: 10 minutes
COOK TIME: 1 hour 20 minutes

Gumbo in a Hurry

    2 cans (14½ ounces *each*) chicken broth

    1 can (14½ ounces) tomatoes, cut up, undrained

    ½ cup *each* minced celery and onion

    ¼ cup FRANK'S® REDHOT® Original Cayenne Pepper Sauce

    2 bay leaves

    1 teaspoon dried thyme leaves

    1 pound medium raw shrimp, peeled and deveined

    1 can (6 ounces) crabmeat, drained

    1 (4-ounce) boneless skinless chicken breast or thigh,
       cut into small cubes

    1 package (10 ounces) frozen sliced okra, thawed

       Hot cooked rice

1. Combine broth, tomatoes, ½ *cup water,* celery, onion, **Frank's RedHot** Sauce, bay leaves and thyme in large saucepan or Dutch oven. Heat to boiling. Stir in shrimp, crabmeat and chicken. Reduce heat to medium-low. Cook, uncovered, 10 minutes; stirring occasionally.

2. Stir in okra. Cook over medium-low heat 5 minutes or until okra is tender. *Do not boil.* Serve gumbo over rice in soup bowls. Serve with crusty French bread or garlic bread, if desired.

Makes 6 servings

PREP TIME: 5 minutes
COOK TIME: 15 minutes

NEW ORLEANS FISH SOUP

1 can (about 15 ounces) cannellini beans, rinsed and drained

1 can (about 14 ounces) reduced-sodium chicken broth

1 yellow squash, halved lengthwise and sliced (1 cup)

1 tablespoon Cajun seasoning

2 cans (about 14 ounces each) no-salt-added stewed tomatoes

1 pound skinless firm fish fillets, such as grouper, cod or haddock, cut into 1-inch pieces

½ cup sliced green onions

1 teaspoon grated orange peel

1. Combine beans, broth, squash and Cajun seasoning in large saucepan; bring to a boil over high heat.

2. Stir in tomatoes and fish; cover and simmer over medium-low heat 3 to 5 minutes or until fish just begins to flake when tested with fork. Stir in green onions and orange peel.

Makes 4 servings

Shrimp & Corn Chowder with Sun-Dried Tomatoes

1   can (10¾ ounces) CAMPBELL'S® Condensed Cream of Potato Soup

1½   cups half-and-half

2   cups whole kernel corn, drained

2   tablespoons sun-dried tomatoes, cut into strips

1   cup small **or** medium peeled and deveined cooked shrimp

2   tablespoons chopped fresh chives

  Ground black pepper

1. Heat the soup, half-and-half, corn and tomatoes in a 3-quart saucepan over medium heat to a boil. Reduce the heat to low. Cook for 10 minutes.

2. Stir in the shrimp and chives and cook until the mixture is hot and bubbling. Season with the black pepper.

Makes 4 servings

KITCHEN TIP: For a lighter version, use skim milk instead of the half-and-half.

PREP TIME: 10 minutes
COOK TIME: 20 minutes
TOTAL TIME: 30 minutes

NO-FUSS
VEGETABLES

SALSA GAZPACHO

  1 jar (16 ounces) ORTEGA® Thick & Chunky Salsa

1½ cups water

  1 cup finely chopped celery

  1 cup diced peeled cucumber

  ½ cup finely chopped green bell pepper

  ½ cup finely chopped red bell pepper

  ¼ cup chopped green onion

  1 can (4 ounces) ORTEGA® Diced Green Chiles

  ½ teaspoon POLANER® Minced Garlic

     Salt and black pepper, to taste

  ¼ cup chopped fresh cilantro (optional)

  1 cup croutons (optional)

COMBINE salsa, water, celery, cucumber, bell peppers, green onion, chiles, garlic, and salt and pepper to taste in large bowl; mix well.

COVER and refrigerate 2 hours. If desired, top with cilantro and croutons before serving.

Makes 6 servings

Easy Mushroom Soup

1¾ cups SWANSON® 50% Less Sodium Beef Broth

1¾ cups SWANSON® Natural Goodness® Chicken Broth

⅛ teaspoon ground black pepper

⅛ teaspoon dried rosemary leaves, crushed

2 cups sliced fresh mushrooms (about 8 ounces)

¼ cup thinly sliced carrot

¼ cup finely chopped onion

¼ cup sliced celery

¼ cup fresh **or** frozen peas

1 tablespoon sliced green onion

1. Heat the beef broth, chicken broth, black pepper, rosemary, mushrooms, carrot, onion, celery and peas in a 4-quart saucepan over medium heat to a boil. Reduce the heat to low. Cover and cook for 15 minutes.

2. Add the green onion. Cook for 5 minutes or until the vegetables are tender.

Makes 4 servings

PREP TIME: 15 minutes
COOK TIME: 25 minutes
TOTAL TIME: 40 minutes

Szechuan Vegetable Soup

2 cans (about 14 ounces each) vegetable broth

2 teaspoons minced garlic

1 teaspoon minced fresh ginger

¼ teaspoon red pepper flakes

1 package (16 ounces) frozen vegetable medley, such as broccoli, carrots, water chestnuts and red bell peppers

1 package (5 ounces) Asian curly noodles or 5 ounces uncooked angel hair pasta, broken in half

3 tablespoons soy sauce

1 tablespoon dark sesame oil

¼ cup thinly sliced green onions

1. Combine broth, garlic, ginger and red pepper flakes in large saucepan; bring to a boil over high heat. Add vegetables and noodles; cover and return to a boil. Reduce heat to medium-low; simmer, uncovered, 5 to 6 minutes or until vegetables and noodles are tender, stirring occasionally.

2. Stir in soy sauce and sesame oil; cook 3 minutes. Stir in green onions just before serving.

Makes 4 servings

NOTE: For a heartier, protein-packed main dish, add 1 package (14 ounces) extra firm tofu, drained and cut into ¾-inch cubes, to the broth mixture with the soy sauce and sesame oil.

AMERICA'S GARDEN SOUP

2 cans (14.5 ounces each) DEL MONTE® Diced Tomatoes with Basil, Garlic and Oregano–No Salt Added

2 cans (14.5 ounces each) COLLEGE INN® Light & Fat Free Chicken Broth 50% Less Sodium

1 can (15.25 ounces) DEL MONTE® Whole Kernel Corn– No Salt Added

1 can (14.5 ounces) DEL MONTE® Cut Green Beans– No Salt Added

1 can (14.5 ounces) DEL MONTE® Zucchini with Italian Style Tomato Sauce

1 can (14.5 ounces) DEL MONTE® Whole New Potatoes, cut into cubes

1 can (8.25 ounces) DEL MONTE® Sliced Carrots

1. Drain liquid from all vegetables, except tomatoes and zucchini.

2. Combine all ingredients in 5-quart saucepan.

3. Bring to boil. Reduce heat and simmer 3 minutes.

Makes 10 servings

Pesto and Tortellini Soup

3 cans (about 14 ounces each) chicken or vegetable broth

1 package (9 ounces) refrigerated cheese tortellini

3 to 4 cups packed stemmed fresh spinach

1 jar (7 ounces) roasted red peppers, drained and thinly sliced

¾ cup frozen green peas

1 to 2 tablespoons pesto

Grated Parmesan cheese

1. Bring broth to a boil in large saucepan over high heat. Add tortellini; return to a boil. Reduce heat to medium; simmer 6 minutes.

2. Stir in spinach, roasted peppers, peas and pesto; simmer 2 minutes or until pasta is tender.

3. Serve with Parmesan.

Makes 6 servings

Pizza Soup

2 cans (10¾ ounces each) condensed tomato soup

¾ teaspoon garlic powder

½ teaspoon dried oregano leaves

¾ cup uncooked tiny pasta shells (¼-inch)

1 cup shredded mozzarella cheese

1 cup FRENCH'S® French Fried Onions

1. Combine soup, *2 soup cans of water,* garlic powder and oregano in small saucepan. Bring to a boil over medium-high heat.

2. Add pasta. Cook 8 minutes or until pasta is tender.

3. Stir in cheese. Cook until cheese melts. Sprinkle with French Fried Onions.

Makes 4 servings

PREP TIME: 5 minutes
COOK TIME: 10 minutes

Souped-Up Soup

    2 cups water

    1 can (10¾ ounces) condensed tomato soup

    1 carrot, peeled and sliced

    ¼ cup uncooked elbow macaroni

    ¼ cup chopped celery

    ¼ cup diced zucchini

    ½ teaspoon dried Italian seasoning

    ½ cup croutons

    2 tablespoons grated Parmesan cheese

1. Combine water, water, carrot, macaroni, celery, zucchini and Italian seasoning in medium saucepan; bring to a boil over medium-high heat. Reduce heat to medium-low; simmer 10 minutes or until macaroni and vegetables are tender.

2. Top with croutons and Parmesan.

Makes 4 servings

Garlic Potato Soup

3½ cups SWANSON® Chicken Broth (Regular, Natural Goodness® **or** Certified Organic)

4 cloves garlic, minced

4 medium red potatoes, cut into cubes (about 4 cups)

2 medium carrots, diced (about 1 cup)

1 medium onion, chopped (about ½ cup)

1 stalk celery, chopped (about ½ cup)

2 slices bacon, cooked and crumbled

1 cup milk

1 cup instant mashed potato flakes **or** buds

1 tablespoon chopped fresh parsley

1. Heat the broth, garlic, potatoes, carrots, onion, celery and bacon in a 4-quart saucepan over medium-high heat to a boil. Reduce the heat to low. Cover and cook for 15 minutes or until the vegetables are tender.

2. Reduce the heat to medium. Stir the milk, potato flakes and parsley in the saucepan. Cook until the mixture is hot and bubbling, stirring occasionally.

Makes 4 servings

PREP TIME: 15 minutes
COOK TIME: 25 minutes
TOTAL TIME: 40 minutes

Italian Tomato and Pasta Soup

  5 cups water

  2 tablespoons dried vegetable flakes, soup greens
     or dehydrated vegetables

  1 tablespoon minced onion

  1 teaspoon sugar

  1 teaspoon chicken bouillon granules

  1 teaspoon dried Italian seasoning

  ½ teaspoon minced garlic

  ¼ teaspoon black pepper

  1 can (about 28 ounces) crushed tomatoes

  3 cups chopped fresh spinach

  2½ cups uncooked farfalle (bow tie) or rotini pasta

  4 to 6 slices bacon, crisp-cooked and crumbled

  ½ cup shredded Parmesan cheese

1. Combine water, vegetable flakes, onion, sugar, bouillon, Italian seasoning, garlic and pepper in large saucepan; bring to a boil over high heat. Boil 10 to 12 minutes.

2. Stir in tomatoes, spinach, pasta and bacon; cook over medium heat 12 to 14 minutes or until pasta is tender. Sprinkle with Parmesan.

Makes 4 to 5 servings

Spinach Tortellini Soup

4 cups SWANSON® Vegetable Broth (Regular **or** Certified Organic

¼ teaspoon garlic powder **or** 1 clove garlic, minced

¼ teaspoon black pepper

¾ cup frozen **or** shelf-stable cheese-filled tortellini (about 3 ounces)

2 cups coarsely chopped fresh spinach leaves

1. Heat the broth, garlic powder and black pepper in a 3-quart saucepan over high heat to a boil.

2. Reduce the heat to medium. Stir in the tortellini. Cook for 10 minutes. Stir in the spinach. Cook for 5 minutes or until the tortellini is tender but still firm.

Makes 6 servings

CURRIED VEGETABLE-RICE SOUP

1 package (16 ounces) frozen stir-fry vegetables

1 can (about 14 ounces) vegetable broth

¾ cup uncooked instant brown rice

2 teaspoons curry powder

½ teaspoon salt

½ teaspoon hot pepper sauce

1 can (14 ounces) unsweetened coconut milk

1 tablespoon lime juice

1. Combine vegetables and broth in large saucepan; bring to a boil over high heat. Stir in rice, curry powder, salt and hot pepper sauce; cover and simmer over medium-low heat 8 minutes or until rice is tender, stirring once.

2. Stir in coconut milk; cook 3 minutes or until heated through. Remove from heat; stir in lime juice. Serve immediately.

Makes 4 servings

TIP: To reduce fat and calories, substitute light unsweetened coconut milk for regular coconut milk.

Taco Soup

  1 can (10¾ ounces) CAMPBELL'S® Condensed Tomato
     Soup
  1 cup milk
  2 tablespoons taco seasoning mix
  1 can (about 4 ounces) diced green chiles
 18 tortilla chips, crumbled
     Shredded Monterey Jack cheese

1. Heat the soup, milk, taco seasoning and chiles in a 2-quart saucepan over medium heat for 10 minutes or until the mixture is hot and bubbling.

2. Divide the tortilla chips between **2** bowls. Pour the soup over the chips. Top with the cheese.

Makes 2 servings

PREP TIME: 5 minutes
COOK TIME: 10 minutes
TOTAL TIME: 15 minutes

QUICK
& CREAMY

SPICY PUMPKIN SOUP

1 can (15 ounces) solid-pack pumpkin

1 can (about 14 ounces) reduced-sodium vegetable
   or chicken broth

½ cup water

1 can (4 ounces) diced green chiles

1 teaspoon ground cumin

½ teaspoon chili powder

¼ teaspoon garlic powder

⅛ teaspoon ground red pepper (optional)

¼ cup sour cream

Chopped fresh cilantro

1. Combine pumpkin, broth, water, chiles, cumin, chili powder, garlic powder and ground red pepper, if desired, in medium saucepan; bring to a boil over high heat. Reduce heat to medium; simmer 5 minutes, stirring occasionally.

2. Top each serving with dollops of sour cream; sprinkle with cilantro.

Makes 4 servings

BAKED POTATO SOUP

3 cans (10¾ ounces each) condensed cream of mushroom soup

4 cups milk

3 cups diced peeled baked potatoes

½ cup cooked crumbled bacon

1 tablespoon fresh thyme leaves or 1 teaspoon dried thyme leaves

Sour cream and shredded Cheddar cheese

1½ cups FRENCH'S® French Fried Onions

1. Combine soup and milk in large saucepan until blended. Stir in potatoes, bacon and thyme. Cook over medium heat 10 to 15 minutes or until heated through, stirring frequently. Season to taste with salt and pepper.

2. Ladle soup into serving bowls. Top each serving with sour cream, cheese and 3 tablespoons French Fried Onions.

Makes 8 servings

PREP TIME: 10 minutes
COOK TIME: 15 minutes

Cheddar Cheese Soup

¼ cup (½ stick) butter or margarine

¼ cup all-purpose flour

2 cans (12 fluid ounces *each*) NESTLÉ® CARNATION®
   Evaporated Milk

1 cup beer or water

2 teaspoons Worcestershire sauce

½ teaspoon dry mustard (optional)

¼ teaspoon cayenne pepper

2 cups (8 ounces) shredded sharp cheddar cheese

   Toppings: crumbled cooked bacon, sliced green onions,
   croutons

MELT butter in large saucepan. Add flour; cook, stirring constantly, until bubbly. Add evaporated milk; bring to a boil, stirring constantly. Reduce heat; stir in beer, Worcestershire sauce, mustard and cayenne pepper. Cook for 10 minutes. Remove from heat. Stir in cheese until melted. Season with salt. Serve with toppings.

Makes 4 servings

PREP TIME: 10 minutes
COOK TIME: 15 minutes

INDONESIAN CURRIED SOUP

 1 can (14 ounces) coconut milk*
 1 can (10¾ ounces) condensed tomato soup
 ¾ cup milk
 3 tablespoons FRANK'S® REDHOT® Original Cayenne
     Pepper Sauce
 1½ teaspoons curry powder

You can substitute 1 cup half-and-half for coconut milk but increase milk to 1½ cups.

1. Combine all ingredients in medium saucepan; stir until smooth.

2. Cook over low heat about 5 minutes or until heated through, stirring occasionally.

Makes 6 servings (4 cups)

PREP TIME: 5 minutes
COOK TIME: 5 minutes

CREAMY QUESO SOUP

1 tablespoon vegetable oil

1 large onion, diced (about 1 cup)

1 jar (16 ounces) PACE® Mexican Four Cheese Salsa con Queso

2 cups SWANSON® Chicken Broth (Regular, Natural Goodness® **or** Certified Organic)

¼ cup milk

Crushed tortilla chips

Chopped green onions

1. Heat the oil in a 2-quart saucepan over medium-high heat. Add the onion and cook for 10 minutes or until the onion is tender.

2. Reduce the heat to low. Stir the salsa con queso, broth and milk in the saucepan and cook for 3 minutes or until the queso mixture is hot. Serve topped with the tortilla chips and green onions.

Makes 5 servings

PREP TIME: 10 minutes
COOK TIME: 15 minutes
TOTAL TIME: 25 minutes

Pumpkin and Gorgonzola Soup

- 1 can (15 ounces) LIBBY'S® 100% Pure Pumpkin
- 1½ cups water
- 2 teaspoons MAGGI® Instant Chicken Flavor Bouillon
- 1 teaspoon ground sage
- 1 can (12 fluid ounces) NESTLÉ® CARNATION® Evaporated Milk
- ¾ cup (3 ounces) crumbled Gorgonzola cheese
- 1 large green onion, finely chopped

COOK pumpkin, water, bouillon and sage in large saucepan over medium-high heat, stirring frequently, until mixture comes to a boil.

STIR in evaporated milk and cheese. Reduce heat to low; cook, stirring frequently, until most of cheese is melted. Sprinkle with green onion before serving. Season with ground black pepper, if desired.

Makes 4 servings

PREP TIME: 10 minutes
COOK TIME: 15 minutes

HEARTY
BEANS

MINESTRONE SOUP

2 cans (about 14 ounces each) vegetable broth

1 can (28 ounces) crushed tomatoes in tomato purée

1 can (about 15 ounces) white beans, rinsed and drained

¾ cup uncooked small shell pasta

1 package (16 ounces) frozen vegetable medley, such as broccoli, green beans, carrots and red peppers

4 to 6 teaspoons pesto

1. Combine broth, tomatoes and beans in large saucepan; bring to a boil over high heat. Stir in pasta; cook 7 minutes.

2. Stir in vegetables; cook until pasta is tender and vegetables are heated through.

3. Spoon about 1 teaspoon pesto in center of each serving

Makes 4 to 6 servings

Picante Black Bean Soup

    1 tablespoon reserved bacon drippings* or olive oil

    1 large onion, chopped

    1 clove garlic, minced

    2 cans (about 15 ounces each) black beans, undrained

    1 can (about 14 ounces) reduced-sodium beef broth

1¼ cups water

    ¾ cup picante sauce, plus additional for serving

    ½ teaspoon salt

    ½ teaspoon dried oregano

    4 slices bacon, crisp-cooked and coarsely chopped*

       Sour cream

When cooking bacon, reserve drippings to use for cooking onion and garlic.

1. Heat bacon drippings in large saucepan over medium-high heat. Add onion and garlic; cook and stir 3 minutes.

2. Stir in beans with liquid, broth, water, ¾ cup picante sauce, salt and oregano. Reduce heat to low; cover and simmer 20 minutes.

3. Sprinkle with bacon; serve with sour cream and additional picante sauce.

Makes 6 to 8 servings

Quick Italian Bean, Tomato and Spinach Soup

2 cans (about 14 ounces each) diced tomatoes with onions

1 can (about 14 ounces) reduced-sodium chicken broth

2 teaspoons sugar

2 teaspoons dried basil

¾ teaspoon Worcestershire sauce

1 can (about 15 ounces) small white beans, rinsed and drained

3 ounces fresh baby spinach

1 tablespoon extra virgin olive oil

1. Combine tomatoes, broth, sugar, basil and Worcestershire sauce in large saucepan; bring to a boil over high heat. Reduce heat to low; simmer 10 minutes.

2. Stir in beans and spinach; cook 5 minutes or until spinach is tender.

3. Stir in oil just before serving.

Makes 4 servings

Black and White Mexican Bean Soup

- 1 tablespoon vegetable oil
- 1 cup chopped onion
- ½ teaspoon POLANER® Minced Garlic
- ¼ cup all-purpose flour
- 1 packet (1.25 ounces) ORTEGA® Taco Seasoning Mix
- 2 cups milk
- 1 can (about 14 ounces) chicken broth
- 1 package (16 ounces) frozen corn
- 1 can (15 ounces) JOAN OF ARC® Great Northern Beans, rinsed, drained
- 1 can (15 ounces) ORTEGA® Black Beans, rinsed, drained
- 1 can (4 ounces) ORTEGA® Fire-Roasted Diced Green Chiles
- 2 tablespoons chopped fresh cilantro

HEAT oil in large pan or Dutch oven over medium-high heat. Add onion and garlic; cook and stir 4 to 5 minutes or until onion is tender.

STIR in flour and seasoning mix; gradually stir in milk until blended.

ADD in broth, corn, beans and green chiles; stir well. Bring to a boil, stirring constantly. Reduce heat to low; simmer 15 minutes or until thickened, stirring occasionally.

STIR in cilantro. Serve warm.

Makes 6 servings

5-Minute Heat-and-Go Soup

  1 can (about 15 ounces) navy beans, rinsed and drained

  1 can (about 14 ounces) diced tomatoes with green
      peppers and onions

  1 cup water

1½ teaspoons dried basil

 ½ teaspoon sugar

 ½ teaspoon chicken bouillon granules

  1 tablespoon extra virgin olive oil

1. Combine beans, tomatoes, water, basil, sugar and chicken bouillon in medium saucepan; bring to a boil over high heat. Reduce heat to low; simmer 5 minutes.

2. Remove from heat; stir in oil just before serving.

Makes 4 servings

Pasta Fagioli

1 jar (1 pound 8 ounces) RAGÚ® Chunky Pasta Sauce

1 can (19 ounces) white kidney beans, rinsed and drained

1 package (10 ounces) frozen chopped spinach, thawed

8 ounces ditalini pasta, cooked and drained (reserve 2 cups pasta water)

1. Combine Pasta Sauce, beans, spinach, pasta and reserved pasta water in 6-quart saucepan; heat through.

2. Season, if desired, with salt, black pepper and grated Parmesan cheese.

Makes 4 servings

PREP TIME: 20 minutes
COOK TIME: 10 minutes

CONTENTS

Deliciously Simple Skillets ⋮ 96

Quick-Fix Casseroles ⋮ 122

One-Pot Wonders ⋮ 148

Slow-Cooker Suppers ⋮ 174

DELICIOUSLY
SIMPLE SKILLETS

SWIRLY NOODLE TACO SKILLET

1 pound ground beef

1 onion, diced (about 1 cup)

1 packet (1.25 ounces) ORTEGA® Taco Seasoning Mix

1 can (7 ounces) ORTEGA® Fire-Roasted Diced Green
   Chilies

1 jar (16 ounces) ORTEGA® Salsa, any variety

½ pound rotini or fusilli pasta, uncooked

   Shredded Cheddar cheese (optional)

BROWN ground beef and onion in large skillet over
medium-high heat 6 to 8 minutes, stirring to break
up meat. Drain fat.

ADD taco seasoning mix, chilies, salsa and 2 cups water;
stir to combine. Add pasta and stir. Reduce heat to low.
Cover and cook 12 to 14 minutes or until pasta is cooked
through. Serve with cheese.

Makes 6 servings

TIP: This dish also makes a great taco filling for ORTEGA®
Yellow Corn Taco Shells or soft flour tortillas.

PREP TIME: 5 minutes
START TO FINISH TIME: 25 minutes

CHICKEN COUSCOUS

1 tablespoon olive oil

8 ounces boneless skinless chicken breasts, cut into 1-inch cubes

4 medium zucchini, sliced

1 can (about 14 ounces) diced tomatoes

1 can (about 14 ounces) reduced-sodium chicken broth

1 teaspoon dried Italian seasoning

1 cup uncooked whole wheat couscous

1. Heat oil in large skillet over medium-high heat. Add chicken; cook and stir 4 minutes or until lightly browned.

2. Add zucchini, tomatoes, broth and Italian seasoning; simmer over low heat 15 minutes, stirring occasionally.

3. Remove from heat. Stir in couscous; cover and let stand 7 minutes. Fluff with fork.

Makes 4 servings

Spanish Rice with Chorizo

4 links Spanish-style chorizo sausage (about 12 ounces), diagonally sliced

1 green bell pepper, diced

1½ cups uncooked instant rice

1 can (about 14 ounces) diced tomatoes with garlic and onions

1 cup chicken broth or water

2 green onions, chopped

Salt and black pepper

1. Cook and stir sausage and bell pepper in large nonstick skillet over medium heat 5 minutes or until bell pepper is tender.

2. Stir in rice, tomatoes, broth and green onions; bring to a boil over high heat. Reduce heat to medium-low; cover and simmer 8 to 10 minutes or until liquid is absorbed and rice is tender. Season with salt and black pepper.

Makes 4 servings

Tip: For a vegetarian version, substitute soy-based sausages for the chorizo and add 1 tablespoon vegetable oil to the skillet with the sausages and bell pepper. Substitute vegetable broth or water for the chicken broth.

Easy Skillet Ravioli

1 package (about 24 ounces) frozen cheese ravioli

2¼ cups water

½ teaspoon salt

1 jar (1 pound 8 ounces) RAGÚ® Chunky Pasta Sauce

¼ cup heavy cream, half-and-half, evaporated milk, milk or nondairy creamer (optional)

1. In 12-inch nonstick skillet, bring ravioli, water and salt to a boil over high heat. Continue boiling, stirring gently to separate ravioli, 5 minutes.

2. Stir in Pasta Sauce. Cook, covered, over medium heat 10 minutes or until ravioli are tender, stirring occasionally. Stir in cream and heat through. Garnish, if desired, with grated Parmesan cheese.

Makes 4 servings

PREP TIME: 5 minutes
COOK TIME: 20 minutes

SOUTHWESTERN TURKEY STEW

1 tablespoon vegetable oil

1 small onion, finely chopped

1 clove garlic, minced

2 cups reduced-sodium chicken broth

2 cups smoked turkey breast, cut into ½-inch pieces

2 cups frozen corn

1 can (about 14 ounces) diced tomatoes

1 package (about 8 ounces) red beans and rice mix

1 to 2 canned chipotle peppers in adobo sauce,
    drained and minced

Chopped green onion (optional)

1. Heat oil in large skillet over medium-high heat. Add onion and garlic; cook and stir 3 minutes or until onion is translucent.

2. Add broth; bring to a boil. Stir in turkey, corn, tomatoes, rice mix and chipotle pepper. Reduce heat to low; cover and cook about 20 minutes or until rice is tender. Let stand 3 minutes. Sprinkle with green onion, if desired.

Makes 4 servings

PICADILLO TACOS

6 ounces ground beef

½ cup chopped green bell pepper

½ teaspoon ground cumin

½ teaspoon chili powder

⅛ teaspoon ground cinnamon

½ cup chunky salsa

1 tablespoon golden raisins

4 (6-inch) corn tortillas, warmed

Toppings: shredded lettuce, shredded Cheddar cheese and chopped tomato

1. Combine ground beef, bell pepper, cumin, chili powder and cinnamon in large nonstick skillet; cook and stir over medium heat until beef is browned.

2. Stir in salsa and raisins; simmer over low heat 5 minutes or until beef is cooked through, stirring occasionally.

3. Divide meat mixture evenly among tortillas; serve with desired toppings.

Makes 2 servings

Skillet Pesto Tortellini

1¼ cups water

1¼ cups milk

1 package (about 1 ounce) creamy pesto sauce mix

1 package (16 ounces) frozen vegetable medley

1 package (12 ounces) frozen tortellini

Dash ground red pepper

½ cup (2 ounces) shredded mozzarella cheese

1. Combine water, milk and sauce mix in large deep skillet; bring to a boil over high heat.

2. Stir in vegetables, tortellini and ground red pepper; return to a boil. Reduce heat to medium-high; cook 8 to 10 minutes or until pasta is tender and sauce has thickened, stirring occasionally. Sprinkle with mozzarella.

Makes 4 servings

SPICY CHICKEN CHILI MAC

    1 can (about 14½ ounces) whole peeled tomatoes, cut up

 2½ cups water

    1 cup PACE® Picante Sauce

    1 tablespoon chili powder

    ¼ teaspoon garlic powder **or** 2 cloves garlic, minced

    ¼ teaspoon salt

    ¾ cup uncooked elbow macaroni

    2 cups cubed cooked chicken or turkey

1. Mix tomatoes, water, picante sauce, chili powder, garlic and salt in a 10-inch skillet over medium-high heat. Heat to a boil. Stir in the macaroni. Cover and cook over low heat for 15 minutes or until macaroni is done, stirring often.

2. Add the chicken and heat through. Garnish with shredded cheese and sour cream, if desired.

Makes 4 servings

TOTAL TIME: 25 minutes

Mexican Casserole with Tortilla Chips

- 2 teaspoons olive oil
- 12 ounces ground turkey
- 1 can (about 14 ounces) stewed tomatoes
- ½ (16-ounce) package frozen bell pepper stir-fry blend, thawed
- ¾ teaspoon ground cumin
- ½ teaspoon salt
- ½ cup (2 ounces) finely shredded sharp Cheddar cheese
- 2 ounces tortilla chips, crushed

1. Heat oil in large skillet over medium heat. Add turkey; cook until no longer pink, stirring to break up meat.

2. Stir in tomatoes, bell peppers, cumin and salt; bring to a boil. Reduce heat to low; cover and simmer 20 minutes or until vegetables are tender. Sprinkle with Cheddar cheese and chips.

Makes 4 servings

VARIATION: Sprinkle chips into a casserole. Spread cooked turkey mixture evenly over the chips and top with cheese.

Skillet Pasta Roma

½ pound Italian sausage, sliced or crumbled

1 large onion, coarsely chopped

1 large clove garlic, minced

2 cans (14.5 ounces each) DEL MONTE® Diced Tomatoes with Basil, Garlic & Oregano

1 can (8 ounces) DEL MONTE® Tomato Sauce

1 cup water

8 ounces uncooked rotini or other spiral pasta

8 mushrooms, sliced (optional)

Grated Parmesan cheese and fresh parsley sprigs (optional)

1. Brown sausage in large skillet. Add onion and garlic. Cook until onion is soft; drain. Stir in undrained tomatoes, tomato sauce, water and pasta.

2. Cover and bring to a boil; reduce heat. Simmer, covered, 25 to 30 minutes or until pasta is tender, stirring occasionally.

3. Stir in mushrooms, if desired; simmer 5 minutes. Serve in skillet garnished with cheese and parsley, if desired.

Makes 4 servings

Sweet and Sour Beef

  1 pound ground beef

  1 small onion, thinly sliced

  2 teaspoons minced fresh ginger

  1 package (16 ounces) frozen Asian-style vegetables

  6 to 8 tablespoons bottled sweet and sour sauce
     or sauce from vegetable mix

    Hot cooked rice

1. Cook beef, onion and ginger in large skillet over medium-high heat 6 to 8 minutes or until beef is browned, stirring to break up meat. Drain fat.

2. Stir in vegetables and sauce; cover and cook 6 to 8 minutes or until vegetables are heated through, stirring occasionally. Serve over rice.

Makes 4 servings

SKILLET SOUTHWEST CHILI

1 pound lean ground beef

2 cans (14.5 ounces each) DEL MONTE® Diced Tomatoes with Onion and Garlic

1 can (15 ounces) low-sodium black or kidney beans, rinsed and drained

1 can (4 ounces) diced green chiles

1 tablespoon chili powder

Green onions or cilantro (optional)

1. Brown beef in large skillet; drain.

2. Add undrained tomatoes, beans, chiles and chili powder; simmer 10 minutes, stirring occasionally. Garnish with green onions, if desired.

Makes 4 servings

PREP TIME: 10 minutes
COOK TIME: 20 minutes
TOTAL TIME: 30 minutes

MUSHROOM AND CHICKEN SKILLET

1 pound boneless skinless chicken breasts, cut into bite-size pieces

1 can (about 14 ounces) chicken broth

¼ cup water

2 cups uncooked instant rice

½ teaspoon dried thyme

8 ounces mushrooms, thinly sliced

1 can (10¾ ounces) cream of celery soup, undiluted

Chopped fresh parsley

1. Combine chicken, broth and water in large skillet; bring to a boil over medium-high heat. Stir in rice and thyme; top with mushrooms. (Do not stir mushrooms into rice.) Cover skillet; turn off heat and let stand 5 minutes.

2. Gently stir in soup; cook over low heat 5 minutes or until heated through. Sprinkle with parsley.

Makes 4 servings

ASIAN BEEF AND VEGETABLES

    1 pound ground beef or turkey

    1 large onion, coarsely chopped

  2½ cups (8 ounces) frozen mixed vegetable medley, such as carrots, broccoli and red peppers, thawed

    2 cloves garlic, minced

    ½ cup stir-fry sauce

    1 can (3 ounces) chow mein noodles

1. Brown beef and onion in large skillet over medium-high heat 6 to 8 minutes, stirring to break up meat. Drain fat.

2. Add vegetables and garlic; cook and stir 2 minutes or until heated through.

3. Stir in stir-fry sauce; cook 30 seconds or until hot. Serve over chow mein noodles.

Makes 4 servings

QUICK-FIX
CASSEROLES

HAM ASPARAGUS GRATIN

1 can (10¾ ounces) CAMPBELL'S® Condensed Cream
   of Asparagus Soup

½ cup milk

¼ teaspoon onion powder

¼ teaspoon ground black pepper

1½ cups cooked cut asparagus

1½ cups cubed cooked ham

2¼ cups corkscrew-shaped pasta (rotini), cooked
   and drained

1 cup shredded Cheddar cheese or Swiss cheese
   (about 4 ounces)

1. Stir the soup, milk, onion powder, black pepper, asparagus, ham, pasta and ½ cup cheese in a 2-quart shallow baking dish.

2. Bake at 400°F. for 25 minutes or until the ham mixture is hot and bubbling. Stir the ham mixture. Sprinkle with the remaining cheese.

3. Bake for 5 minutes or until the cheese is melted.

Makes 4 servings

Shrimp and Chicken Paella

¾ cup cooked rice

2 cans (about 14 ounces each) diced tomatoes, divided

½ teaspoon ground turmeric *or* ⅛ teaspoon saffron threads

12 ounces medium raw shrimp, peeled and deveined (with tails on)

2 chicken tenders (about 4 ounces), cut into 1-inch pieces

1 cup frozen peas

1. Preheat oven to 400°F. Spray 8-inch square baking dish with nonstick cooking spray. Spread rice in prepared dish.

2. Pour one can of tomatoes over rice; sprinkle with turmeric. Arrange shrimp and chicken over tomatoes; top with peas. Drain remaining can of tomatoes, discarding juice. Spread tomatoes evenly over shrimp and chicken.

3. Cover and bake 30 minutes. Let stand, covered, 5 minutes before serving.

Makes 4 servings

Hearty Potato and Sausage Bake

- 1 pound new red potatoes, cut into halves or quarters
- 1 onion, sliced
- 8 ounces baby carrots
- 2 tablespoons butter, melted
- 1 teaspoon salt
- 1 teaspoon garlic powder
- ½ teaspoon dried thyme
- ½ teaspoon black pepper
- 1 pound cooked chicken sausage or turkey sausage, cut into ¼-inch slices

1. Preheat oven to 400°F. Spray 13×9-inch baking dish with nonstick cooking spray.

2. Combine potatoes, onion, carrots, butter, salt, garlic powder, thyme and pepper in prepared baking dish; toss to coat.

3. Bake 30 minutes. Add sausage; mix well. Bake 15 to 20 minutes or until potatoes are tender and golden brown.

Makes 4 to 6 servings

Creamy Tortellini with Chicken

2 cups PREGO® Fresh Mushroom Italian Sauce

⅓ cup half-and-half

1 package (16 ounces) frozen cheese-filled tortellini, cooked and drained

2 cups cooked chicken strips

1 cup shredded mozzarella cheese (4 ounces)

¼ cup grated Parmesan cheese

1. Stir the Italian sauce and half-and-half in an 11×8-inch (2-quart) shallow baking dish.

2. Add the tortellini, chicken and ½ **cup** of the mozzarella cheese. Stir well to coat. Top with the Parmesan cheese and remaining mozzarella cheese.

3. Bake at 400°F. for 20 minutes or until hot.

Makes 4 servings

EASY SUBSTITUTION TIP: Substitute 1 cup coarsely chopped mushrooms and Prego® Traditional Sauce for the Prego® Fresh Mushroom Italian Sauce.

PREP TIME: 15 minutes
BAKE TIME: 20 minutes

Beef in Wine Sauce

4 pounds boneless beef chuck roast, cut into 1½- to 2-inch pieces

2 cans (10¾ ounces each) condensed golden mushroom soup, undiluted

1 can (8 ounces) sliced mushrooms, drained

¾ cup dry sherry

2 tablespoons garlic powder

1 package (1 ounce) dry onion soup mix

1 bag (20 ounces) frozen sliced carrots, thawed

1. Preheat oven to 325°F. Spray 4-quart casserole with nonstick cooking spray.

2. Combine beef, soup, mushrooms, sherry, garlic powder and dry soup mix in prepared casserole; mix well.

3. Cover and bake 3 hours or until beef is tender. Stir in carrots during last 15 minutes of cooking.

Makes 6 to 8 servings

Easy Chicken & Biscuits

1 can (10¾ ounces) CAMPBELL'S® Condensed Cream of Broccoli Soup (Regular or 98% Fat Free)

1 can (10¾ ounces) CAMPBELL'S® Condensed Cream of Potato Soup

⅔ cup milk

½ teaspoon poultry seasoning

⅛ teaspoon ground black pepper

2 cups frozen mixed vegetables

2 cups cubed cooked chicken or turkey

1 package refrigerated buttermilk biscuits (10 biscuits)

1. Stir the soups, milk, poultry seasoning, black pepper, vegetables and chicken in a 2-quart shallow baking dish.

2. Bake at 400°F. for 20 minutes or until the chicken mixture is hot and bubbling. Cut each biscuit into quarters. Stir the chicken mixture. Top with the biscuits.

3. Bake for 15 minutes or until the biscuits are golden brown.

Makes 4 servings

KITCHEN TIP: Substitute Campbell's® Condensed Cream of Celery Soup for the Cream of Broccoli.

PREP TIME: 10 minutes
BAKE TIME: 35 minutes
TOTAL TIME: 45 minutes

Baked Halibut Casserole

4 fresh or thawed frozen halibut steaks (1 inch thick, about 6 ounces each), rinsed

Salt and black pepper to taste

1 can (8 ounces) tomato sauce

1 package (12 ounces) frozen mixed vegetables such as broccoli, peas, onions and bell peppers

Hot cooked rice (optional)

1. Preheat oven to 350°F. Place halibut in 13×9-inch baking pan; season with salt and pepper.

2. Top fish with tomato sauce and mixed vegetables; season with salt and pepper.

3. Bake 25 to 30 minutes or until fish just begins to flake when tested with fork. Serve over rice, if desired.

Makes 4 servings

E-Z Chicken Tortilla Bake

1 can (10¾ ounces) condensed tomato soup, undiluted

1 cup ORTEGA® Thick & Chunky Salsa

½ cup milk

2 cups cubed cooked chicken

8 (8-inch) ORTEGA® Flour Soft Tortillas, cut into 1-inch pieces

1 cup (4 ounces) shredded Cheddar cheese, divided

PREHEAT the oven to 400°F. Mix soup, salsa, milk, chicken, tortillas and ½ cup cheese in 2-quart shallow baking dish. Cover; bake 30 minutes or until hot. Top with remaining ½ cup cheese.

Makes 4 servings

TIP: Use turkey instead of chicken for an E-Z Turkey Tortilla Bake.

TIP: Two whole chicken breasts (about 10 ounces each) will yield about 2 cups of chopped cooked chicken.

PREP TIME: 10 minutes
START TO FINISH TIME: 40 minutes

Creamy Shrimp and Vegetable Casserole

1 pound fresh or thawed frozen shrimp, peeled and deveined

1 can (10¾ ounces) condensed cream of celery soup, undiluted

½ cup sliced fresh or thawed frozen asparagus (1-inch pieces)

½ cup sliced mushrooms

¼ cup diced red bell pepper

¼ cup sliced green onions

1 clove garlic, minced

¾ teaspoon dried thyme

¼ teaspoon black pepper

Hot cooked rice or orzo (optional)

1. Preheat oven to 375°F. Spray 2-quart baking dish with nonstick cooking spray.

2. Combine shrimp, soup, asparagus, mushrooms, bell pepper, green onions, garlic, thyme and black pepper in prepared baking dish.

3. Cover and bake 30 minutes. Serve over rice, if desired.

Makes 4 servings

CHEESY TUNA NOODLE CASSEROLE

1 can (10¾ ounces) CAMPBELL'S® Condensed Cream of Mushroom Soup (Regular or 98% Fat Free)

½ cup milk

1 cup frozen peas

2 cans (about 6 ounces each) tuna, drained and flaked

2 cups hot cooked medium egg noodles

½ cup shredded Cheddar cheese

1. Stir the soup, milk, peas, tuna and noodles in a 1½-quart casserole.

2. Bake at 400°F. for 20 minutes or until hot. Stir.

3. Sprinkle cheese over the tuna mixture. Bake for 2 minutes more or until the cheese melts.

Makes 4 servings

KITCHEN TIP: Substitute your family's favorite frozen vegetable for the peas.

PREP TIME: 10 minutes
BAKE TIME: 22 minutes

Carolina Baked Beans & Pork Chops

2 cans (16 ounces each) pork and beans

½ cup chopped onion

½ cup chopped green bell pepper

¼ cup packed light brown sugar

¼ cup FRENCH'S® Classic Yellow® Mustard

2 tablespoons FRENCH'S® Worcestershire Sauce

1 tablespoon FRANK'S® REDHOT® Original Cayenne
   Pepper Sauce

6 boneless pork chops (1 inch thick)

1. Preheat oven to 400°F. Combine all ingredients *except pork chops* in 3-quart shallow baking dish; mix well. Arrange pork chops on top, turning once to coat with sauce.

2. Bake, uncovered, 30 to 35 minutes or until pork is no longer pink in center. Stir beans around chops once during baking. Serve with green beans or mashed potatoes, if desired.

Makes 6 servings

PREP TIME: 10 minutes
COOK TIME: 30 minutes

CREAMY CHICKEN AND RICE BAKE

  1 can (12 fluid ounces) NESTLÉ® CARNATION® Evaporated Milk

  1 package (3 ounces) cream cheese, softened

  1 can (10¾ ounces) cream of chicken soup

  ½ cup water

  ½ teaspoon garlic powder

  ⅛ teaspoon ground black pepper

  1 bag (16 ounces) frozen broccoli, cauliflower and carrot mix, thawed

  2 cups cubed cooked chicken

  1½ cups uncooked instant white rice

  ½ cup (2 ounces) shredded cheddar cheese

PREHEAT oven to 350°F. Grease 13×9-inch baking dish.

COMBINE evaporated milk and cream cheese in baking dish with wire whisk until smooth. Add soup, water, garlic powder and black pepper; mix well. Add vegetables, chicken and rice. Cover tightly with foil.

BAKE for 35 minutes. Uncover; top with cheese. Bake for an additional 10 to 15 minutes or until cheese is melted and mixture is bubbly. Let stand 5 minutes before serving.

Makes 8 to 10 servings

PREP TIME: 15 minutes
BAKE TIME: 45 minutes

Easy Chicken Chalupas

    8 (8-inch) flour tortillas
    3 cups shredded cooked chicken (from 1 rotisserie
       chicken)
    2 cups (8 ounces) shredded Cheddar cheese
    1 cup mild green salsa
    1 cup mild red salsa

1. Preheat oven to 350°F. Spray 13×9-inch baking dish with nonstick cooking spray.

2. Place two tortillas in bottom of prepared baking dish, overlapping slightly. Layer tortillas with ¾ cup chicken, ½ cup cheese and ¼ cup of each salsa. Repeat layers three times.

3. Bake 25 minutes or until bubbly and heated through.

Makes 6 servings

> TIP: Serve this easy main dish with toppings such as sour cream, chopped cilantro, sliced black olives, sliced green onions and sliced avocado.

CREAMY 3-CHEESE PASTA

1 can (10¾ ounces) CAMPBELL'S® Condensed Cream of Mushroom Soup (Regular or 98% Fat Free)

1 package (8 ounces) shredded two-cheese blend (about 2 cups)

⅓ cup grated Parmesan cheese

1 cup milk

¼ teaspoon ground black pepper

3 cups corkscrew-shaped pasta (rotini), cooked and drained

1. Stir the soup, cheeses, milk and black pepper in a 1½-quart casserole. Stir in the pasta.

2. Bake at 400°F. for 20 minutes or until the pasta mixture is hot and bubbling.

Makes 4 servings

PREP TIME: 20 minutes
BAKE TIME: 20 minutes
TOTAL TIME: 40 minutes

ONE-POT
WONDERS

SHRIMP AND PEPPER NOODLE BOWL

- 4 cups water
- 2 packages (3 ounces each) shrimp-flavored ramen noodles
- 8 ounces frozen cooked medium shrimp *or* 1 package (8 ounces) frozen cooked baby shrimp
- 1 cup frozen bell pepper strips
- ¼ cup chopped green onions
- 1 tablespoon soy sauce
- ½ teaspoon hot pepper sauce
- 2 tablespoons chopped fresh cilantro (optional)

1. Bring water to a boil in large saucepan over high heat. Reserve seasoning packets from noodles. Break up noodles; add to boiling water. Add shrimp and bell pepper; cook 3 minutes.

2. Stir in seasoning packets, green onions, soy sauce and hot pepper sauce; cook 1 minute. Sprinkle with cilantro, if desired.

Makes 4 servings

Chicken Florentine in Minutes

    3 cups water

    1 cup milk

    2 tablespoons butter

    2 packages (about 4 ounces each) fettuccine Alfredo
        or stroganoff pasta mix

   ¼ teaspoon black pepper

    1 package (about 10 ounces) refrigerated fully cooked
        chicken breast strips, cut into ½-inch pieces

    4 cups baby spinach, coarsely chopped

   ¼ cup diced roasted red pepper

   ¼ cup sour cream

1. Bring water, milk and butter to a boil in large saucepan over medium-high heat. Stir in pasta mix and black pepper. Reduce heat to medium; cook 8 minutes or until pasta is tender, stirring occasionally.

2. Stir in chicken, spinach and roasted pepper; cook 2 minutes or until heated through. Remove from heat; stir in sour cream.

Makes 4 servings

SIMPLE TURKEY CHILI

1 pound ground turkey

1 small onion, chopped

1 can (about 28 ounces) diced tomatoes

1 can (about 15 ounces) chickpeas, rinsed and drained

1 can (about 15 ounces) kidney beans, rinsed and drained

1 can (about 15 ounces) black beans, rinsed and drained

1 can (6 ounces) tomato sauce

1 can (4 ounces) chopped green chiles

1 to 2 tablespoons chili powder

1. Cook turkey and onion in large saucepan over medium-high heat until turkey is cooked through, stirring to break up turkey. Drain fat.

2. Stir in tomatoes, chickpeas, beans, tomato sauce, chiles and chili powder; bring to a boil over high heat. Reduce heat to medium-low; simmer about 20 minutes, stirring occasionally.

Makes 8 servings

Italian Sausage and Vegetable Stew

1 pound hot or mild Italian sausage links, cut into 1-inch pieces

1 package (16 ounces) frozen vegetable blend, such as onions and bell peppers

2 medium zucchini, sliced

1 can (about 14 ounces) Italian-style diced tomatoes

1 can (4 ounces) sliced mushrooms, drained

4 cloves garlic, minced

1. Brown sausage in large saucepan over medium-high heat 5 minutes, stirring frequently. Drain fat.

2. Add frozen vegetables, zucchini, tomatoes, mushrooms and garlic; bring to a boil. Reduce heat to medium-low; cover and simmer 10 minutes. Uncover; cook 5 to 10 minutes or until thickened slightly.

Makes 6 servings

Tortellini-Vegetable Toss

1 jar (24 ounces) PREGO® Chunky Garden Combination Italian Sauce

1 bag (16 ounces) frozen vegetable combination (broccoli, cauliflower, carrots)

1 package (16 ounces) frozen cheese-filled tortellini, cooked and drained

Grated Parmesan cheese

1. Heat the Italian sauce in a 3-quart saucepan over medium heat to a boil. Stir in the vegetables. Cover and cook for 10 minutes or until the vegetables are tender-crisp, stirring occasionally.

2. Put the tortellini in a large serving bowl. Pour the vegetable mixture over the tortellini. Toss to coat. Serve with the cheese.

Makes 4 servings

PREP TIME: 5 minutes
COOK TIME: 15 minutes
TOTAL TIME: 20 minutes

SPANISH SEAFOOD STEW

  2 jars (16 ounces each) PACE® Picante Sauce

  1 bottle (8 ounces) clam juice

  ¼ cup dry white wine or water

  1 package (3½ ounces) chorizo sausage, sliced

  2½ pounds cod, haddock or snapper

  24 littleneck clams

  Hot cooked regular long-grain white rice

1. Heat picante sauce, clam juice and wine in a 6-quart saucepan over high heat to a boil. **Cover.** Add chorizo, fish and clams.

2. Reduce heat to low and cook for 10 minutes or until done. Serve over rice.

Makes 8 servings

TOTAL TIME: 25 minutes

Bow Tie Pasta Bowl

    3 cups reduced-sodium chicken broth

    6 ounces uncooked bow tie pasta

    ⅛ teaspoon red pepper flakes

    1½ cups diced cooked chicken

    1 medium tomato, seeded and diced

    1 cup packed spring greens or spinach, coarsely chopped

    3 tablespoons chopped fresh basil

    ½ teaspoon salt

    1 cup (4 ounces) shredded mozzarella cheese

    2 tablespoons grated Parmesan cheese

1. Bring broth to boil in large saucepan over high heat. Add pasta and red pepper flakes; return to a boil. Reduce heat to medium-low; cover and simmer 10 minutes or until pasta is tender.

2. Add chicken; cook 1 minute. Remove from heat; stir in tomato, greens, basil and salt. Top with mozzarella and Parmesan.

Makes 4 servings

CHILI Á LA MEXICO

    2 pounds ground beef

    2 cups finely chopped onions

    2 cloves garlic, minced

    1 can (28 ounces) whole peeled tomatoes, undrained,
       coarsely chopped

    1 can (6 ounces) tomato paste

  1½ to 2 tablespoons chili powder

    1 teaspoon ground cumin

    ¼ teaspoon salt

    ¼ teaspoon ground red pepper

    ¼ teaspoon ground cloves (optional)

       Lime wedges and cilantro sprigs (optional)

1. Brown beef in large saucepan over medium-high heat 6 to
8 minutes, stirring to separate meat. Drain fat. Add onions and
garlic; cook and stir over medium heat 5 minutes or until onions
are softened.

2. Stir in tomatoes with juice, tomato paste, chili powder,
cumin, salt, red pepper and cloves, if desired; bring to a
boil over high heat. Reduce heat to low; cover and simmer
30 minutes, stirring occasionally. Serve with lime wedges
and cilantro, if desired.

Makes 6 to 8 servings

CURRIED SHRIMP AND NOODLES

    3 cups water

    2 packages (about 1.6 ounces each) instant curry-
       flavored rice noodle soup mix

    1 package (8 ounces) frozen cooked baby shrimp

    1 cup frozen bell pepper strips, cut into 1-inch pieces
       or 1 cup frozen peas

    ¼ cup chopped green onions

    ¼ teaspoon salt

    ¼ teaspoon black pepper

    1 to 2 tablespoons fresh lime juice

1. Bring water to a boil in large saucepan over high heat. Add soup mixes, shrimp, bell pepper, green onions, salt and black pepper; cook 3 to 5 minutes or until noodles are tender, stirring frequently.

2. Stir in lime juice. Serve immediately.

Makes 4 servings

Asian Vegetables and Ham

2 cups reduced-sodium chicken broth

1 package (16 ounces) frozen stir-fry vegetables

1 teaspoon sesame oil

4 ounces thinly sliced ham, cut into ½-inch pieces

2 cups uncooked instant white long grain rice

Soy sauce (optional)

1. Combine broth, vegetables and sesame oil in large saucepan; bring to a boil over high heat.

2. Remove from heat; stir in ham and rice. Cover and let stand 5 minutes. Serve with soy sauce, if desired.

Makes 4 servings

VARIATION: Substitute 12 ounces cooked chicken for the ham.

Pesto Turkey & Pasta

¼ cup milk

1 tablespoon margarine or butter

1 (4.7-ounce) package PASTA RONI® Chicken & Broccoli Flavor with Linguine

1 pound boneless, skinless turkey or chicken breasts, cut into thin strips

1 medium red or green bell pepper, sliced

½ medium onion, chopped

½ cup prepared pesto sauce

¼ cup pine nuts or chopped walnuts, toasted

Grated Parmesan cheese (optional)

1. In large saucepan, bring 1½ cups water, milk and margarine to a boil. Stir in pasta and Special Seasonings. Reduce heat to medium. Gently boil 1 minute.

2. Add turkey, bell pepper and onion. Return to a boil. Gently boil 8 to 9 minutes or until pasta is tender and turkey is no longer pink inside, stirring occasionally.

3. Stir in pesto. Let stand 3 to 5 minutes before serving. Sprinkle with nuts and cheese, if desired.

Makes 4 servings

TIP: To make your own pesto, blend 2 cups fresh parsley or basil, 2 cloves garlic and ⅓ cup walnuts in a blender or food processor. Slowly add ½ cup olive oil and ¼ cup Parmesan cheese.

PREP TIME: 10 minutes
COOK TIME: 20 minutes

SAUSAGE BEAN STEW

1 pound cooked smoked sausage, cut into ¼-inch slices, halved

1 can (15.5 ounces) JOAN OF ARC® Great Northern Beans, rinsed, drained

1 can (15 ounces) ORTEGA® Black Beans, rinsed, drained

1 can (15 ounces) lima beans, drained

1 can (11 ounces) whole kernel corn, drained

1 can (10 ounces) ORTEGA® Fire-Roasted Diced Green Chiles

1 can (10 ounces) diced tomatoes

½ teaspoon salt

⅛ teaspoon black pepper

Hot cooked rice (optional)

COMBINE all ingredients except rice in large saucepan. Cook over medium heat until heated through. Serve over rice, if desired.

Makes 6 servings

PREP TIME: 10 minutes
START TO FINISH TIME: 20 minutes

Confetti Chicken Chili

2 teaspoons olive oil

1 pound ground chicken or turkey

1 large onion, chopped

3½ cups reduced-sodium chicken broth

1 can (about 15 ounces) Great Northern beans, rinsed and drained

2 carrots, chopped

1 medium green bell pepper, chopped

2 plum tomatoes, chopped

1 jalapeño pepper,* finely chopped (optional)

2 teaspoons chili powder

½ teaspoon ground red pepper

Jalapeño peppers can sting and irritate the skin, so wear rubber gloves when handling peppers and do not touch your eyes.

1. Heat oil in large saucepan over medium heat. Add chicken and onion; cook and stir 5 minutes or until chicken is browned. Drain fat.

2. Stir in broth, beans, carrots, bell pepper, tomatoes, jalapeño, if desired, chili powder and red pepper; bring to a boil over high heat. Reduce heat to low; cover and simmer 15 minutes.

Makes 5 servings

Shrimp Alfredo with Sugar Snap Peas

½ cup milk

3 tablespoons margarine or butter

1 (4.7-ounce) package PASTA RONI® Fettuccine Alfredo

1 (9-ounce) package frozen sugar snap peas, thawed

8 ounces cooked, deveined, peeled medium shrimp

½ teaspoon ground lemon pepper

1. In large saucepan, bring 1¼ cups water, milk, margarine, pasta and Special Seasonings to a boil. Reduce heat to low. Gently boil 4 minutes, stirring occasionally.

2. Stir in snap peas, shrimp and lemon pepper; cook 1 to 2 minutes or until pasta is tender. Let stand 3 minutes before serving.

Makes 4 servings

TIP: If you don't have lemon pepper in your cupboard, try Italian seasoning instead.

PREP TIME: 5 minutes
COOK TIME: 15 minutes

JERK TURKEY STEW

    1 tablespoon vegetable oil

    1 small red onion, chopped

    1 clove garlic, minced

    ½ teaspoon ground ginger

    ¼ teaspoon salt

    ¼ teaspoon black pepper

    ⅛ teaspoon ground red pepper

    ⅛ teaspoon ground allspice

    1 can (about 28 ounces) diced tomatoes

    3 cups diced cooked turkey

    2 cups diced cooked sweet potatoes (½-inch pieces)

    ½ cup turkey broth or gravy

    1 tablespoon lime juice

    1 tablespoon minced fresh chives

1. Heat oil in large saucepan over medium heat. Add onion and garlic; cook and stir 5 minutes. Add ginger, salt, black pepper, red pepper and allspice; cook 20 seconds. Stir in tomatoes, turkey, sweet potatoes and broth. Reduce heat to low; simmer 15 minutes.

2. Stir in lime juice; cover and let stand 10 minutes. Sprinkle with chives just before serving.

Makes 4 servings

SLOW-COOKER
SUPPERS

SLOW COOKER SOUTHWESTERN PORK ROAST

2½ pounds boneless pork roast

1 envelope LIPTON® Recipe Secrets® Onion Soup Mix

1 can (14½ ounces) diced tomatoes, undrained

2 cans (4 ounces each) chopped green chilies, undrained

3 tablespoons firmly packed brown sugar

2 teaspoons chili powder

1 teaspoon ground cumin

1. In slow cooker, arrange pork. Combine LIPTON® Recipe Secrets® Onion Soup Mix with remaining ingredients; pour over pork.

2. Cook, covered, on low 8 to 10 hours or on high 4 to 6 hours or until pork is tender. Serve, if desired, with hot cooked noodles or rice.

Makes 8 servings

PREP TIME: 5 minutes
COOK TIME: 4 hours (High)

Easy Italian Chicken

4 boneless skinless chicken breasts
  (about 4 ounces each)

8 ounces mushrooms, sliced

1 medium onion, chopped

1 medium green bell pepper, chopped

1 medium zucchini, diced

1 jar (26 ounces) pasta sauce

  Hot cooked pasta (optional)

1. Combine chicken, mushrooms, onion, bell pepper, zucchini and pasta sauce in slow cooker.

2. Cover; cook on LOW 6 to 8 hours or until chicken is tender. Serve over pasta, if desired.

Makes 4 servings

THREE-BEAN MOLE CHILI

1 can (about 15 ounces) chili beans in spicy sauce

1 can (about 15 ounces) pinto beans, rinsed and drained

1 can (about 15 ounces) black beans, rinsed and drained

1 can (about 14 ounces) Mexican- or chili-style diced tomatoes

1 large green bell pepper, diced

1 small onion, diced

½ cup beef, chicken or vegetable broth

¼ cup prepared mole paste*

2 teaspoons ground cumin

2 teaspoons chili powder

2 teaspoons ground coriander (optional)

2 teaspoons minced garlic

Toppings: crushed tortilla chips, chopped cilantro or shredded cheese

Mole paste is available in the Mexican aisle of large supermarkets or in specialty markets.

1. Combine beans, tomatoes, bell pepper, onion, broth, mole paste, cumin, chili powder, coriander, if desired, and garlic in slow cooker.

2. Cover; cook on LOW 5 to 6 hours. Serve with desired toppings.

Makes 4 to 6 servings

SUPER-EASY BEEF BURRITOS >

  1 boneless beef chuck roast (2 to 3 pounds)

  1 can (28 ounces) enchilada sauce

  4 (8-inch) flour tortillas

     Toppings: shredded cheese, sour cream, salsa, shredded lettuce and chopped tomatoes

1. Place roast in slow cooker; cover with enchilada sauce.

2. Cover; cook on LOW 6 to 8 hours or until beef begins to fall apart. Shred beef; serve in tortillas with desired toppings.

Makes 4 servings

HARVEST HAM SUPPER

  6 carrots, cut into 2-inch pieces

  3 medium sweet potatoes, quartered

  1 to 1½ pounds boneless ham

  1 cup maple syrup

1. Place carrots and sweet potatoes in bottom of slow cooker. Place ham on top of vegetables. Pour syrup over ham and vegetables.

2. Cover; cook on LOW 6 to 8 hours.

Makes 6 servings

CLASSIC CHICKEN & RICE

3 cans (10¾ ounces each) condensed cream of chicken soup, undiluted

2 cups uncooked instant rice

1 cup water

1 pound boneless skinless chicken breasts or chicken breast tenders

½ teaspoon salt

¼ teaspoon paprika

¼ teaspoon black pepper

½ cup diced celery

1. Combine soup, rice and water in slow cooker. Add chicken; sprinkle with salt, paprika and pepper. Sprinkle celery over chicken.

2. Cover; cook on LOW 6 to 8 hours or on HIGH 3 to 4 hours.

Makes 4 servings

Slow-Cooked Autumn Brisket

1 boneless beef brisket (about 3 pounds)

1 small head cabbage (about 1 pound), cut into 8 wedges

1 large sweet potato (about ¾ pound), peeled and cut into 1-inch pieces

1 large onion, cut into 8 wedges

1 medium Granny Smith apple, cored and cut into 8 wedges

2 cans (10¾ ounces each) CAMPBELL'S® Condensed Cream of Celery Soup (Regular or 98% Fat Free)

1 cup water

2 teaspoons caraway seed (optional)

1. Place the brisket in a 6-quart slow cooker. Top with the cabbage, sweet potato, onion and apple. Stir the soup, water and caraway seed, if desired, in a small bowl. Pour the soup mixture over the brisket and vegetable mixture.

2. Cover and cook on LOW for 8 to 9 hours* or until the brisket is fork-tender. Season as desired.

*Or on HIGH for 4 to 5 hours.

Makes 8 servings

PREP TIME: 20 minutes
COOK TIME: 8 hours
TOTAL TIME: 8 hours 20 minutes

New World Pork Stew

2 small sweet potatoes (about ¾ pound), peeled and cut into 2-inch pieces

1 package (10 ounces) frozen corn

1 package (9 ounces) frozen cut green beans

1 cup chopped onion

1¼ pounds pork stew meat, cut into 1-inch cubes

1 can (about 14 ounces) diced tomatoes

¼ cup water

1 to 2 tablespoons chili powder

½ teaspoon salt

½ teaspoon ground coriander

1. Place sweet potatoes, corn, green beans and onion in slow cooker. Top with pork. Add tomatoes, water, chili powder, salt and coriander.

2. Cover; cook on LOW 7 to 9 hours.

Makes 6 servings

MEATBALLS IN BURGUNDY SAUCE

60 frozen fully cooked meatballs, partially thawed
   and separated

3 cups chopped onions

1½ cups water

1 cup Burgundy or other red wine

¼ cup ketchup

2 packages (about 1 ounce each) beef gravy mix

1 tablespoon dried oregano

Hot cooked egg noodles (optional)

1. Combine meatballs, onions, water, wine, ketchup, gravy mix and oregano in slow cooker.

2. Cover; cook on HIGH 4 to 5 hours. Serve over noodles, if desired.

Makes 6 to 8 servings

PACIFIC ISLAND CHICKEN & RICE

2 cans (10½ ounces each) CAMPBELL'S® Condensed Chicken Broth

1 cup water

¼ cup soy sauce

2 cloves garlic, minced

8 skinless, boneless chicken thighs (about 2 pounds), cut into 1½-inch pieces

1 medium green or red pepper, cut into 1½-inch pieces (about 1 cup)

4 green onions, cut into 2-inch pieces (about 1 cup)

1 can (20 ounces) pineapple chunks in juice, undrained

1 cup uncooked regular long-grain white rice

Toasted sliced almonds

1. Stir the broth, water, soy sauce, garlic, chicken, pepper, onions, pineapple with juice and rice in 6-quart slow cooker.

2. Cover and cook on LOW for 7 to 8 hours* or until chicken is cooked through.

3. Sprinkle with the almonds before serving.

*Or on HIGH for 4 to 5 hours.

Makes 8 servings

KITCHEN TIP: To toast almonds, arrange almonds in single layer in a shallow baking pan. Bake at 350°F. for 10 minutes or until lightly browned.

PREP TIME: 20 minutes
COOK TIME: 7 hours

CARIBBEAN SWEET POTATO AND BEAN STEW

2 medium sweet potatoes (about 1 pound), peeled and cut into 1-inch cubes

2 cups frozen cut green beans

1 can (about 15 ounces) black beans, rinsed and drained

1 can (about 14 ounces) vegetable broth

1 small onion, sliced

2 teaspoons Caribbean jerk seasoning

½ teaspoon dried thyme

¼ teaspoon salt

¼ teaspoon ground cinnamon

⅓ cup slivered almonds, toasted*

Hot pepper sauce (optional)

To toast almonds, spread in single layer on baking sheet. Bake in preheated 350°F oven 8 to 10 minutes or until golden brown, stirring frequently.

1. Combine sweet potatoes, green beans, black beans, broth, onion, jerk seasoning, thyme, salt and cinnamon in slow cooker.

2. Cover; cook on LOW 5 to 6 hours or until vegetables are tender. Serve with almonds and hot pepper sauce, if desired.

Makes 4 servings

SLOW COOKER SAUSAGE AND PEPPERS

    1 envelope LIPTON® Recipe Secrets® Onion Soup Mix
    4 medium green bell peppers, sliced (about 4 cups)
  1½ pounds sweet Italian sausage links
    1 can (8 ounces) tomato sauce
    ½ teaspoon dried oregano leaves, crushed

1. In slow cooker, combine LIPTON® Recipe Secrets® Onion Soup Mix with rest of ingredients.

2. Cook, covered, on low 8 to 10 hours or on high 4 to 6 hours, or until sausage is done. Serve over hot cooked pasta or in hero rolls.

Makes 4 servings

PREP TIME: 15 minutes
COOK TIME: 4 hours (High)

Pork with Mustard and Sauerkraut ›

 2 jars (32 ounces each) sauerkraut, rinsed and drained
 2½ cups water
 3 tablespoons brown mustard
 1 package (1 ounce) dry onion soup mix
 3 pounds boneless pork loin roast

1. Combine sauerkraut, water, mustard and soup mix in slow cooker; mix well. Top with pork.

2. Cover; cook on LOW 8 hours. Slice pork; serve with sauerkraut.

Makes 6 servings

Mushroom-Beef Stew

 1 pound beef stew meat
 1 can (10¾ ounces) condensed cream of mushroom soup, undiluted
 2 cans (4 ounces each) sliced mushrooms, drained
 1 package (1 ounce) dry onion soup mix
   Hot cooked noodles

1. Combine beef, condensed soup, mushrooms and soup mix in slow cooker.

2. Cover; cook on LOW 8 to 10 hours. Serve over noodles.

Makes 4 servings

BEEF BOURGUIGNONNE

1 can (10¾ ounces) CAMPBELL'S® Condensed Golden
  Mushroom Soup

1 cup Burgundy or other dry red wine

2 cloves garlic, minced

1 teaspoon dried thyme leaves, crushed

2 cups small button mushrooms (about 6 ounces)

2 cups fresh or thawed frozen baby carrots

1 cup frozen small whole onions, thawed

1½ pounds beef top round steak, 1½-inches thick,
   cut into 1-inch pieces

1. Stir the soup, wine, garlic, thyme, mushrooms, carrots, onions and beef in a 3½-quart slow cooker.

2. Cover and cook on LOW for 8 to 9 hours* or until the beef is fork-tender.

*Or on HIGH for 4 to 5 hours.

Makes 6 servings

PREP TIME: 10 minutes
COOK TIME: 8 hours

No-Fuss Macaroni and Cheese

2 cups (about 8 ounces) uncooked elbow macaroni

4 ounces pasteurized process cheese product, cubed

1 cup (4 ounces) shredded Cheddar cheese

½ teaspoon salt

⅛ teaspoon black pepper

1½ cups milk

1. Combine macaroni, cheeses, salt and pepper in slow cooker. Pour milk over top.

2. Cover; cook on LOW 2 to 3 hours, stirring after 20 to 30 minutes.

Makes 6 to 8 servings

VARIATION: Stir in sliced hot dogs or vegetables near the end of cooking. Cover; cook until heated through.

NOTE: As with all macaroni and cheese dishes, the cheese sauce thickens and begins to dry out as it sits. If it becomes too dry, stir in a little extra milk. Do not cook longer than 4 hours.

CONTENTS

Classic Dump Cakes ⋮ 200

Family Favorites ⋮ 228

Fall Flavors ⋮ 254

Acknowledgments ⋮ 280

Index ⋮ 281

CLASSIC
Dump Cakes

Peach Melba Dump Cake

2 cans (21 ounces each) peach pie filling

1 package (12 ounces) frozen raspberries, thawed and drained

1 package (about 15 ounces) yellow cake mix

½ cup (1 stick) butter, cut into thin slices

Ice cream (optional)

1. Preheat oven to 350°F. Spray 13×9-inch baking pan with nonstick cooking spray.

2. Spread peach pie filling in prepared pan; sprinkle with raspberries. Top with cake mix, spreading evenly. Top with butter in single layer, covering cake mix as much as possible.

3. Bake 40 to 45 minutes or until toothpick inserted into center of cake comes out clean. Cool at least 15 minutes before serving. Serve with ice cream, if desired.

Makes 12 to 16 servings

DOUBLE PINEAPPLE BERRY CAKE

1 can (20 ounces) crushed pineapple, undrained

1 package (12 ounces) frozen mixed berries, thawed and drained

1 package (about 18 ounces) pineapple cake mix

½ cup (1 stick) butter, cut into thin slices

Whipped cream (optional)

1. Preheat oven to 350°F. Spray 13×9-inch baking pan with nonstick cooking spray.

2. Spread pineapple and berries in prepared pan. Top with cake mix, spreading evenly. Top with butter in single layer, covering cake mix as much as possible.

3. Bake 45 to 50 minutes or until toothpick inserted into center of cake comes out clean. Cool at least 15 minutes before serving. Serve with whipped cream, if desired.

Makes 12 to 16 servings

Simple S'more Cake

   1 package (about 15 ounces) milk chocolate cake mix

   1 package (4-serving size) chocolate instant pudding and pie filling mix

1½ cups milk

   1 package (10 ounces) mini marshmallows

   1 cup milk chocolate chips *or* 2 (4-ounce) milk chocolate bars, broken into pieces

   5 whole graham crackers, broken into bite-size pieces

1. Preheat oven to 350°F. Spray 13×9-inch baking pan with nonstick cooking spray.

2. Combine cake mix, pudding mix and milk in large bowl; beat 1 to 2 minutes or until well blended. Spread batter in prepared pan.

3. Bake 30 to 35 minutes or until toothpick inserted into center comes out clean. *Turn oven to broil.*

4. Sprinkle marshmallows, chocolate chips and graham crackers over cake. Broil 6 inches from heat source 30 seconds to 1 minute or until marshmallows are golden brown. Cool at least 15 minutes before serving.

Makes 12 to 16 servings

Banana Split Cake

1 can (20 ounces) crushed pineapple, undrained

1 can (14½ ounces) tart cherries in water, drained

1 package (about 18 ounces) banana cake mix

½ cup (1 stick) butter, cut into thin slices

½ cup semisweet chocolate chips

½ cup chopped pecans

Whipped cream and maraschino cherries (optional)

1. Preheat oven to 350°F. Spray 13×9-inch baking pan with nonstick cooking spray.

2. Spread pineapple and tart cherries in prepared pan. Top with cake mix, spreading evenly. Top with butter in single layer, covering cake mix as much as possible. Sprinkle with chocolate chips and pecans.

3. Bake 55 to 60 minutes or until toothpick inserted into center of cake comes out clean. Cool at least 15 minutes before serving. Top with whipped cream and maraschino cherries, if desired.

Makes 12 to 16 servings

APPLE PEACH DUMP CAKE

2 cans (21 ounces each) apple pie filling

2 cans (15 ounces each) peach slices, drained

1 teaspoon ground cinnamon, divided

½ teaspoon ground nutmeg, divided

1 package (about 15 ounces) white cake mix

½ cup (1 stick) butter, melted

1. Preheat oven to 350°F. Spray 13×9-inch baking pan with nonstick cooking spray.

2. Spread apple pie filling and peaches in prepared pan. Sprinkle with ½ teaspoon cinnamon and ¼ teaspoon nutmeg. Top with cake mix, spreading evenly. Pour butter over top, covering cake mix as much as possible. Sprinkle with remaining ½ teaspoon cinnamon and ¼ teaspoon nutmeg.

3. Bake 1 hour or until top is lightly browned and toothpick inserted into center of cake comes out clean. Cool at least 15 minutes before serving.

Makes 12 to 16 servings

PINEAPPLE ANGEL CAKE

    2 cups fresh or thawed frozen sliced strawberries

    1 can (20 ounces) crushed pineapple, undrained

    1 package (16 ounces) angel food cake mix

1. Preheat oven to 350°F.

2. Spread strawberries in 13×9-inch baking pan. Combine pineapple and cake mix in large bowl; beat 1 to 2 minutes or until well blended. Spread batter evenly over strawberries.

3. Bake 35 to 40 minutes or until toothpick inserted into center comes out clean. Cool in pan at least 30 minutes before serving.

Makes 12 to 16 servings

SUPER FRUITY CONFETTI CAKE

   2 cans (15 ounces each) fruit cocktail, drained

   1 package (about 15 ounces) white cake mix

  ½ cup (1 stick) butter, cut into thin slices

  ¼ cup multicolored tiny crunchy tangy candies

1. Preheat oven to 350°F. Spray 13×9-inch baking pan with nonstick cooking spray.

2. Spread fruit cocktail in prepared pan. Top with cake mix, spreading evenly. Top with butter in single layer, covering cake mix as much as possible.

3. Bake 45 to 50 minutes or until toothpick inserted into center of cake comes out clean, sprinkling with candies during last 20 minutes of baking. Cool at least 15 minutes before serving.

Makes 12 to 16 servings

ORANGE PINEAPPLE COCONUT CAKE

    1 can (20 ounces) crushed pineapple, undrained
    1 can (15 ounces) mandarin oranges in light syrup,
       drained
  1½ cups flaked coconut, divided
    1 package (about 15 ounces) vanilla cake mix
    ½ cup (1 stick) butter, cut into thin slices

1. Preheat oven to 350°F. Spray 13×9-inch baking pan with nonstick cooking spray.

2. Spread pineapple and mandarin oranges in prepared pan; sprinkle with ½ cup coconut. Top with cake mix, spreading evenly. Top with butter in single layer, covering cake mix as much as possible. Sprinkle with remaining 1 cup coconut.

3. Bake 45 to 50 minutes or until toothpick inserted into center of cake comes out clean. Cool at least 15 minutes before serving.

Makes 12 to 16 servings

Pink Lemonade Cake

  3 cups fresh or thawed frozen sliced strawberries

  ¼ cup powdered pink lemonade mix

  1 package (about 15 ounces) white cake mix

  ½ cup (1 stick) butter, cut into thin slices

  ½ cup water

1. Preheat oven to 350°F. Spray 9-inch square baking pan with nonstick cooking spray.

2. Spread strawberries in prepared pan; sprinkle with lemonade mix. Top with cake mix, spreading evenly. Top with butter in single layer. Slowly pour water over top, covering cake mix as much as possible.

3. Bake 40 to 45 minutes or until toothpick inserted into center of cake comes out clean. Cool at least 15 minutes before serving.

Makes 9 servings

PEACH STRAWBERRY CAKE

    1 can (29 ounces) peach slices in light syrup, undrained
  1½ cups frozen sliced strawberries, thawed and drained
    1 package (about 15 ounces) yellow cake mix
    ½ cup (1 stick) butter, melted
       Ice cream (optional)

1. Preheat oven to 350°F. Spray 13×9-inch baking pan with nonstick cooking spray.

2. Spread peaches and strawberries in prepared pan. Top with cake mix, spreading evenly. Pour butter over top, covering cake mix as much as possible.

3. Bake 50 to 55 minutes or until toothpick inserted into center of cake comes out clean. Cool at least 15 minutes before serving. Serve with ice cream, if desired.

Makes 12 to 16 servings

MIXED BERRY DUMP CAKE

   2 packages (12 ounces each) frozen mixed berries,
      thawed and drained

   1 package (about 15 ounces) white cake mix

   ¼ teaspoon ground cinnamon

   1 can (12 ounces) lemon-lime soda

   ½ cup cinnamon chips

1. Preheat oven to 350°F. Spray 13×9-inch baking pan with nonstick cooking spray.

2. Spread mixed berries in prepared pan. Top with cake mix, spreading evenly. Sprinkle with cinnamon. Slowly pour soda over top, covering cake mix as much as possible. Sprinkle with cinnamon chips.

3. Bake 45 to 50 minutes or until toothpick inserted into center of cake comes out clean. Cool at least 15 minutes before serving.

Makes 12 to 16 servings

Cha-Cha-Cha Cherry Cake

2 packages (12 ounces each) frozen cherries,
  thawed and drained

1 package (4-serving size) cherry gelatin

1 package (about 15 ounces) white cake mix

½ cup (1 stick) butter, cut into thin slices

1 cup chopped walnuts

¼ cup water

1. Preheat oven to 350°F. Spray 9-inch square baking pan with nonstick cooking spray.

2. Spread cherries in prepared pan; sprinkle with gelatin. Top with cake mix, spreading evenly. Top with butter in single layer, covering cake mix as much as possible. Sprinkle with walnuts. Drizzle water over top.

3. Bake 50 to 60 minutes or until toothpick inserted into center of cake comes out clean. Cool at least 15 minutes before serving.

Makes 9 servings

TROPICAL DUMP CAKE

1 can (20 ounces) crushed pineapple, undrained

1 can (15 ounces) peach slices in light syrup, undrained

1 package (about 15 ounces) yellow cake mix

½ cup (1 stick) butter, cut into thin slices

1 cup packed brown sugar

½ cup flaked coconut

½ cup chopped pecans

1. Preheat oven to 350°F. Spray 13×9-inch pan with nonstick cooking spray.

2. Spread pineapple and peaches in prepared pan. Top with cake mix, spreading evenly. Top with butter in single layer, covering cake mix as much as possible. Sprinkle with brown sugar, coconut and pecans.

3. Bake 40 to 45 minutes or until toothpick inserted into center of cake comes out clean. Cool at least 15 minutes before serving.

Makes 12 to 16 servings

BLUEBERRY CINNAMON CAKE

2 packages (12 ounces each) frozen blueberries, thawed and drained

⅓ cup sugar

¾ teaspoon ground cinnamon, divided

1 package (about 15 ounces) yellow cake mix

¾ cup (1½ sticks) butter, cut into thin slices

Ice cream (optional)

1. Preheat oven to 350°F. Spray 13×9-inch baking pan with nonstick cooking spray.

2. Spread blueberries in prepared pan. Sprinkle with sugar and ½ teaspoon cinnamon; toss to coat. Top with cake mix, spreading evenly. Top with butter in single layer, covering cake mix as much as possible. Sprinkle with remaining ¼ teaspoon cinnamon.

3. Bake 50 to 60 minutes or until toothpick inserted into center of cake comes out clean. Cool at least 15 minutes before serving. Serve with ice cream, if desired.

Makes 12 to 16 servings

Super Strawberry Cake

3 cups thawed frozen or fresh strawberries, cut into halves or quarters

1 package (about 15 ounces) strawberry cake mix

½ cup (1 stick) butter, cut into thin slices

Whipped cream (optional)

1. Preheat oven to 350°F. Spray 13×9-inch baking pan with nonstick cooking spray.

2. Spread strawberries in prepared pan. Top with cake mix, spreading evenly. Top with butter in single layer, covering cake mix as much as possible.

3. Bake 45 to 50 minutes or until toothpick inserted into center of cake comes out clean. Cool at least 15 minutes before serving. Serve with whipped cream, if desired.

Makes 12 to 16 servings

FAMILY
FAVORITES

CHERRY CHEESECAKE DUMP CAKE

1 can (21 ounces) cherry pie filling

1 can (14½ ounces) tart cherries in water, drained

4 ounces cream cheese, cut into small pieces

1 package (about 15 ounces) yellow cake mix

½ cup (1 stick) butter, cut into thin slices

1. Preheat oven to 350°F. Spray 13×9-inch baking pan with nonstick cooking spray.

2. Spread cherry pie filling and tart cherries in prepared pan. Scatter cream cheese pieces over cherries. Top with cake mix, spreading evenly. Top with butter in single layer, covering cake mix as much as possible.

3. Bake 45 to 50 minutes or until toothpick inserted into center of cake comes out clean. Cool at least 15 minutes before serving.

Makes 12 to 16 servings

Tempting Turtle Cake

1 package (about 15 ounces) devil's food cake mix

1 package (4-serving size) chocolate instant pudding and pie filling mix

1½ cups milk

1 cup chopped caramels

1 cup semisweet chocolate chips

½ cup pecan pieces

½ teaspoon coarse salt (optional)

1. Preheat oven to 350°F. Spray 13×9-inch baking pan with nonstick cooking spray.

2. Combine cake mix, pudding mix and milk in large bowl; beat 1 to 2 minutes or until well blended. Spread batter in prepared pan; top with caramels, chocolate chips and pecans. Sprinkle with salt, if desired.

3. Bake 30 to 35 minutes or until toothpick inserted into center comes out clean. Cool at least 15 minutes before serving.

Makes 12 to 16 servings

APRICOT DOUBLE CHIP CAKE

2 cups apricot preserves or jam

½ cup semisweet chocolate chips, divided

½ cup white chocolate chips, divided

1 package (about 15 ounces) yellow cake mix

½ cup (1 stick) butter, cut into thin slices

⅓ cup water

1. Preheat oven to 350°F. Spray 9-inch square baking pan with nonstick cooking spray.

2. Spread preserves in prepared pan. Sprinkle with half of semisweet chips and half of white chips. Top with cake mix, spreading evenly. Top with butter in single layer, covering cake mix as much as possible. Drizzle water over top. Sprinkle with remaining semisweet and white chips.

3. Bake 50 to 55 minutes or until toothpick inserted into center of cake comes out clean. Cool at least 15 minutes before serving.

Makes 9 servings

RED VELVET WHITE CHIP CAKE

        1 package (about 18 ounces) red velvet cake mix
        1 package (4-serving size) vanilla instant pudding
            and pie filling mix
    1½ cups milk
        2 ounces cream cheese, cut into small pieces
      ½ cup white chocolate chips

1. Preheat oven to 350°F. Spray 13×9-inch baking pan with nonstick cooking spray.

2. Combine cake mix, pudding mix and milk in medium bowl; beat 1 to 2 minutes or until well blended. Spread batter in prepared pan; sprinkle with cream cheese and white chips.

3. Bake 25 to 30 minutes or until toothpick inserted into center comes out clean. Cool in pan on wire rack. Serve warm or at room temperature.

Makes 12 to 16 servings

Raspberry Lovers' Dump Cake

1 can (21 ounces) raspberry pie filling

1 package (12 ounces) frozen raspberries, thawed and drained

1 package (12 ounces) semisweet chocolate chips, divided

1 package (about 15 ounces) white cake mix

¾ cup (1½ sticks) butter, cut into thin slices

½ cup packed brown sugar

Ice cream (optional)

1. Preheat oven to 350°F. Spray 13×9-inch baking pan with nonstick cooking spray.

2. Spread raspberry pie filling in prepared pan; sprinkle with raspberries. Sprinkle with half of chocolate chips. Top with cake mix, spreading evenly. Top with butter in single layer, covering cake mix as much as possible. Sprinkle with brown sugar and remaining chocolate chips.

3. Bake 50 to 60 minutes or until golden brown and toothpick inserted into center of cake comes out clean. Cool at least 15 minutes before serving. Serve with ice cream, if desired.

Makes 12 to 16 servings

Caramel Candy Cake

    1 package (about 15 ounces) yellow cake mix

    2 eggs

    ½ cup (1 stick) butter, melted

    ½ cup milk

    1 package (8 ounces) unwrapped bite-size chocolate peanut caramel candies, chopped, divided

    2 tablespoons caramel topping, warmed

1. Preheat oven to 350°F. Spray 9-inch square baking pan with nonstick cooking spray.

2. Combine cake mix, eggs, butter and milk in large bowl; beat 1 to 2 minutes or until well blended. Stir in half of candy. Spread batter in prepared pan; sprinkle with remaining candy. Drizzle with caramel topping.

3. Bake 30 to 35 minutes or until toothpick inserted into center comes out clean. Cool in pan at least 15 minutes before serving.

Makes 9 servings

BLACK FOREST CAKE

2 cans (21 ounces each) cherry pie filling

1 package (about 15 ounces) chocolate fudge
   cake mix

¾ cup semisweet chocolate chips

¾ cup (1½ sticks) butter, melted

1. Preheat oven to 350°F. Spray 13×9-inch baking pan
with nonstick cooking spray.

2. Spread cherry pie filling in prepared pan. Top with cake
mix, spreading evenly. Sprinkle with chocolate chips. Pour
butter over top, covering cake mix as much as possible.

3. Bake 30 to 35 minutes or until toothpick inserted
into center of cake comes out clean. Cool at least
15 minutes before serving.

Makes 12 to 16 servings

BANANA STRAWBERRY DUMP CAKE

1 can (21 ounces) strawberry pie filling

1 can (20 ounces) crushed pineapple, undrained

1 package (about 18 ounces) banana cake mix

½ cup (1 stick) butter, cut into thin slices

1. Preheat oven to 350°F. Spray 13×9-inch baking pan with nonstick cooking spray.

2. Spread strawberry pie filling and pineapple in prepared pan. Top with cake mix, spreading evenly. Top with butter in single layer, covering cake mix as much as possible.

3. Bake 45 to 50 minutes or until toothpick inserted into center of cake comes out clean. Cool at least 15 minutes before serving.

Makes 12 to 16 servings

Blackberry Almond Cake

2 packages (12 ounces each) frozen blackberries, thawed and drained

¼ cup granulated sugar

1 package (about 15 ounces) yellow cake mix

¾ cup (1½ sticks) butter, cut into thin slices

½ cup sliced almonds

¼ cup packed brown sugar

1. Preheat oven to 350°F. Spray 13×9-inch baking pan with nonstick cooking spray.

2. Spread blackberries in prepared pan; sprinkle with granulated sugar and toss to coat. Top with cake mix, spreading evenly. Top with butter in single layer, covering cake mix as much as possible. Sprinkle with almonds and brown sugar.

3. Bake 50 to 60 minutes or until toothpick inserted into center of cake comes out clean. Cool at least 15 minutes before serving.

Makes 12 to 16 servings

LEMON BLUEBERRY CAKE

1 package (about 18 ounces) lemon cake mix

1 package (4-serving size) lemon instant pudding and pie filling mix

4 eggs

¾ cup water

½ cup vegetable or canola oil

1 cup fresh blueberries, divided

1. Preheat oven to 350°F. Spray 13×9-inch baking pan with nonstick cooking spray.

2. Combine cake mix, pudding mix, eggs, water and oil in large bowl; beat 1 to 2 minutes or until well blended. Gently fold in ½ cup blueberries. Spread batter in prepared pan; sprinkle with remaining ½ cup blueberries.

3. Bake 20 to 25 minutes or until toothpick inserted into center comes out clean. Cool completely in pan on wire rack.

Makes 12 to 16 servings

ISLAND DELIGHT CAKE

     3 ripe mangoes, peeled and cubed (about 4½ cups)

     1 package (about 18 ounces) pineapple cake mix

     1 can (12 ounces) lemon-lime or orange soda

     ½ cup chopped macadamia nuts (optional)

1. Preheat oven to 350°F. Spray 13×9-inch baking pan with nonstick cooking spray.

2. Spread mangoes in prepared pan. Top with cake mix, spreading evenly. Pour soda over top, covering cake mix as much as possible. Sprinkle with macadamia nuts, if desired.

3. Bake 35 to 40 minutes or until toothpick inserted into center of cake comes out clean. Cool at least 15 minutes before serving.

Makes 12 to 16 servings

Rainbow Dump Cake

   1 **can (20 ounces) crushed pineapple, undrained**

   1 **can (14½ ounces) tart cherries in water, drained**

   1 **package (about 15 ounces) yellow cake mix**

  ½ **cup (1 stick) butter, cut into thin slices**

  ½ **cup candy-coated chocolate pieces**

1. Preheat oven to 350°F. Spray 13×9-inch baking pan with nonstick cooking spray.

2. Spread pineapple and cherries in prepared pan. Top with cake mix, spreading evenly. Top with butter in single layer, covering cake mix as much as possible.

3. Bake 35 to 40 minutes or until toothpick inserted into center of cake comes out clean, sprinkling with chocolate pieces during last 10 minutes of baking. Cool at least 15 minutes before serving.

Makes 12 to 16 servings

PEACH CRANBERRY UPSIDE DOWN CAKE

¼ cup (½ stick) butter, melted

½ cup packed brown sugar

3 cups thawed frozen or canned peach slices (thick slices cut in half)

2 cups fresh or thawed frozen cranberries

1 package (about 15 ounces) yellow cake mix, plus ingredients to prepare mix

1. Preheat oven to 350°F. Spray two 9-inch round cake pans with nonstick cooking spray.

2. Divide butter and brown sugar between prepared pans; spread evenly over bottom of pans. Arrange peach slices over butter mixture; sprinkle with cranberries.

3. Prepare cake mix according to package directions. Spread batter over fruit in each pan.

4. Bake 30 to 35 minutes or until toothpick inserted into center of cakes comes out clean. Cool 5 minutes; invert cakes onto serving plates. Cool at least 30 minutes before serving.

Makes 12 to 16 servings

DOUBLE BANANA CAKE

1 package (about 18 ounces) banana cake mix, plus 1 package (about 18 ounces) banana cake mix, plus ingredients to prepare mix

¾ cup chopped hazelnuts or sliced almonds, toasted,* divided

1 banana, thinly sliced

¼ cup chocolate hazelnut spread, warmed**

To toast hazelnuts, spread in single layer on baking sheet. Bake in preheated 350°F oven 5 to 7 minutes or until golden brown, stirring frequently.

**Microwave on LOW (30%) about 1 minute or until pourable.*

1. Preheat oven to 350°F. Spray 9-inch square baking pan with nonstick cooking spray.

2. Prepare cake mix according to package directions; stir in ½ cup hazelnuts. Spread half of batter in prepared pan. Top with banana slices; drizzle with 2 tablespoons chocolate hazelnut spread. Top with remaining half of batter; sprinkle with remaining ¼ cup hazelnuts and drizzle with 2 tablespoons chocolate hazelnut spread.

3. Bake 25 to 30 minutes or until toothpick inserted into center comes out clean. Cool in pan at least 15 minutes before serving.

Makes 9 servings

FALL
FLAVORS

CRANBERRY APPLE CAKE

- 1 can (21 ounces) apple pie filling
- 1 can (14 ounces) whole berry cranberry sauce
- 1 package (about 15 ounces) yellow cake mix
- ½ cup (1 stick) butter, cut into thin slices
- ½ cup chopped walnuts

1. Preheat oven to 350°F. Spray 13×9-inch baking pan with nonstick cooking spray.

2. Spread apple pie filling in prepared pan; top with cranberry sauce. Top with cake mix, spreading evenly. Top with butter in single layer, covering cake mix as much as possible. Sprinkle with walnuts.

3. Bake 50 to 55 minutes or until toothpick inserted into center of cake comes out clean. Cool at least 15 minutes before serving.

Makes 12 to 16 servings

PUMPKIN PECAN CAKE

  1 can (15 ounces) solid-pack pumpkin

  1 can (12 ounces) evaporated milk

  1 cup packed brown sugar

  3 eggs

  2 teaspoons pumpkin pie spice

  ½ teaspoon salt

  1 package (about 15 ounces) yellow cake mix

  ¾ cup (1½ sticks) butter, cut into thin slices

  ½ cup pecan halves

1. Preheat oven to 350°F. Spray 13×9-inch baking pan with nonstick cooking spray.

2. Combine pumpkin, evaporated milk, brown sugar, eggs, pumpkin pie spice and salt in large bowl; beat until well blended. Pour into prepared pan. Top with cake mix, spreading evenly. Top with butter in single layer, covering cake mix as much as possible. Sprinkle with pecans.

3. Bake about 1 hour or until toothpick inserted into center of cake comes out clean. Cool completely in pan on wire rack.

Makes 18 servings

Granola Caramel Carrot Cake

1 can (20 ounces) crushed pineapple, undrained

1 package (about 15 ounces) carrot cake mix

½ cup (1 stick) butter, cut into thin slices

1 cup granola

3 tablespoons caramel topping, warmed

Ice cream (optional)

1. Preheat oven to 350°F. Spray 13×9-inch baking pan with nonstick cooking spray.

2. Spread pineapple in prepared pan. Top with cake mix, spreading evenly. Top with butter in single layer, covering cake mix as much as possible. Sprinkle with granola; drizzle with caramel topping.

3. Bake 50 to 55 minutes or until toothpick inserted into center of cake comes out clean. Cool at least 15 minutes before serving. Serve with ice cream, if desired.

Makes 12 to 16 servings

Sweet Potato Cake

  1 can (29 ounces) sweet potatoes, drained

  1 package (about 15 ounces) yellow cake mix

  3 eggs

1½ teaspoons apple pie spice, plus additional
      for top of cake

  ⅔ cup chopped nuts, divided

1. Preheat oven to 350°F. Spray 13×9-inch baking pan with nonstick cooking spray.

2. Place sweet potatoes in large bowl; mash with fork. Add cake mix, eggs and apple pie spice; beat 1 to 2 minutes or until well blended. Stir in ⅓ cup nuts. Spread batter in prepared pan; sprinkle with remaining ⅓ cup nuts and additional apple pie spice.

3. Bake 30 to 35 minutes or until toothpick inserted into center comes out clean. Cool in pan at least 15 minutes before serving.

Makes 12 to 16 servings

ORANGE CRANBERRY CAKE

  1 package (about 15 ounces) yellow cake mix

  4 eggs

  ¾ cup orange juice

  ½ cup vegetable or canola oil

  ¼ cup water

  1 cup dried cranberries

     Powdered sugar (optional)

1. Preheat oven to 350°F. Grease and flour 12-cup (10-inch) bundt pan.

2. Combine cake mix, eggs, orange juice, oil and water in large bowl; beat 1 to 2 minutes or until well blended. Stir in cranberries. Pour batter into prepared pan.

3. Bake about 40 minutes or until toothpick inserted near center comes out clean. Cool in pan 10 minutes; invert onto wire rack to cool completely.

4. Sprinkle with powdered sugar just before serving, if desired.

Makes 12 servings

SWEET-HOT APPLE DUMP CAKE

2 cans (21 ounces each) apple pie filling

¼ cup plus 2 tablespoons hot cinnamon candies, divided

1 package (about 15 ounces) yellow cake mix

½ cup (1 stick) butter, cut into thin slices

1. Preheat oven to 350°F. Spray 13×9-inch baking pan with nonstick cooking spray.

2. Spread apple pie filling in prepared pan. Sprinkle with ¼ cup cinnamon candies. Top with cake mix, spreading evenly. Top with butter in single layer, covering cake mix as much as possible.

3. Bake 45 to 55 minutes or until toothpick inserted into center of cake comes out clean, sprinkling with remaining 2 tablespoons cinnamon candies during last 10 minutes of baking. Cool at least 15 minutes before serving.

Makes 12 to 16 servings

TRIPLE GINGER PEAR CAKE

  2 cans (29 ounces each) pear slices in light syrup, undrained

  ⅓ cup finely chopped crystallized ginger

  ¼ teaspoon ground ginger

  1 package (about 15 ounces) yellow cake mix

  ½ cup (1 stick) butter, cut into thin slices

  1 cup crumbled gingersnaps (about 16 cookies)

1. Preheat oven to 350°F. Spray 13×9-inch baking pan with nonstick cooking spray.

2. Drain pears, reserving 1 cup syrup. Cut pear slices into ¾-inch chunks with paring knife or scissors. Combine pears and reserved syrup in prepared pan; sprinkle with crystallized ginger and ground ginger. Top with cake mix, spreading evenly. Top with butter in single layer, covering cake mix as much as possible. Sprinkle with gingersnap crumbs.

3. Bake 40 to 45 minutes or until toothpick inserted into center of cake comes out clean. Cool at least 15 minutes before serving.

Makes 12 to 16 servings

CRANBERRY COBBLER CAKE

1 can (14 ounces) whole berry cranberry sauce

1 package (9 ounces) yellow cake mix

¼ cup (½ stick) butter, melted

½ cup granola

1. Preheat oven to 350°F. Spray 9-inch pie plate with nonstick cooking spray.

2. Spread cranberries in prepared pie plate. Top with cake mix, spreading evenly. Pour butter over top, covering cake mix as much as possible. Sprinkle with granola.

3. Bake 55 to 60 minutes or until toothpick inserted into center of cake comes out clean. Cool at least 15 minutes before serving.

Makes 6 to 8 servings

APPLE PIE DUMP CAKE

    1 can (21 ounces) apple pie filling
    1 package (about 15 ounces) white cake mix
    3 eggs
    ½ cup vegetable or canola oil
    ⅓ cup chopped pecans

1. Preheat oven to 350°F. Spray 13×9-inch baking pan with nonstick cooking spray.

2. Place apple pie filling in large bowl; cut apple slices into chunks with paring knife or scissors. Add cake mix, eggs and oil; beat 1 to 2 minutes or until well blended. Spread batter in prepared pan; sprinkle with pecans.

3. Bake 40 to 45 minutes or until toothpick inserted into center comes out clean. Cool in pan at least 15 minutes before serving.

Makes 12 to 16 servings

CARAMEL APPLE PEANUT CAKE

    2 cans (21 ounces each) apple pie filling
    ½ cup lightly salted peanuts, divided
    1 package (about 15 ounces) yellow cake mix
    ½ cup (1 stick) butter, cut into thin slices
    ⅓ cup caramel topping, warmed

1. Preheat oven to 350°F. Spray 13×9-inch baking pan with nonstick cooking spray.

2. Spread apple pie filling in prepared pan; sprinkle with ¼ cup peanuts. Top with cake mix, spreading evenly. Top with butter in single layer, covering cake mix as much as possible. Drizzle with caramel topping; sprinkle with remaining ¼ cup peanuts.

3. Bake 35 to 40 minutes or until toothpick inserted into center of cake comes out clean. Cool at least 15 minutes before serving.

Makes 12 to 16 servings

CRANBERRY PEAR SPICE CAKE

  1 can (29 ounces) pear slices in light syrup, undrained

  1 package (12 ounces) fresh or thawed frozen cranberries

  1 package (about 15 ounces) spice cake mix

  ½ cup (1 stick) butter, cut into thin slices

  1 cup chopped walnuts

     Whipped cream (optional)

1. Preheat oven to 350°F. Spray 13×9-inch baking pan with nonstick cooking spray.

2. Drain ½ cup syrup from pears. Pour remaining pears and syrup into prepared pan; cut pears into 1-inch pieces with paring knife or scissors. Spread cranberries over pears. Top with cake mix, spreading evenly. Top with butter in single layer, covering cake mix as much as possible. Sprinkle with walnuts.

3. Bake 40 to 45 minutes or until toothpick inserted into center of cake comes out clean. Cool at least 15 minutes before serving. Serve with whipped cream, if desired.

Makes 12 to 16 servings

Carrot Banana Cake

  1 package (about 15 ounces) carrot cake mix,
     plus ingredients to prepare mix

  1 teaspoon baking soda

  2 bananas, mashed (about 1 heaping cup)

  1 cup chopped walnuts

  ½ cup raisins

     Prepared cream cheese frosting, warmed (optional)

     Additional chopped walnuts (optional)

1. Preheat oven to 350°F. Grease and flour 12-cup (10-inch) bundt pan.

2. Prepare cake mix according to package directions. Stir baking soda into mashed bananas; add to batter and beat until well blended. Stir in 1 cup walnuts and raisins. Pour into prepared pan.

3. Bake 40 to 45 minutes or until toothpick inserted near center comes out clean. Cool in pan 10 minutes; invert onto wire rack to cool completely.

4. Drizzle cream cheese frosting over cooled cake and sprinkle with additional walnuts, if desired.

Makes 12 servings

AUTUMN DUMP CAKE

1 can (29 ounces) pear slices in light syrup, undrained

1 can (21 ounces) apple pie filling

½ cup dried cranberries

1 package (about 15 ounces) yellow cake mix

½ cup (1 stick) butter, cut into thin slices

¼ cup caramel topping, warmed

1. Preheat oven to 350°F. Spray 13×9-inch baking pan with nonstick cooking spray.

2. Drain pears, reserving ½ cup syrup. Spread pears and apple pie filling in prepared pan; drizzle with reserved syrup. Sprinkle with cranberries. Top with cake mix, spreading evenly. Top with butter in single layer, covering cake mix as much as possible. Drizzle with caramel topping.

3. Bake 40 to 45 minutes or until toothpick inserted into center of cake comes out clean. Cool at least 15 minutes before serving.

Makes 12 to 16 servings

Pumpkin Chocolate Chip Cake

   1 package (about 15 ounces) spice cake mix

   1 can (15 ounces) solid-pack pumpkin

   2 eggs

  ⅓ cup water

   1 cup semisweet chocolate chips

   1 cup semisweet chocolate chips, melted (optional)

1. Preheat oven to 350°F. Grease and flour 12-cup (10-inch) bundt pan.

2. Combine cake mix, pumpkin, eggs and water in large bowl; beat 1 to 2 minutes or until well blended. Stir in 1 cup chocolate chips. Pour batter into prepared pan.

3. Bake 35 to 40 minutes or until toothpick inserted near center comes out clean. Cool in pan 10 minutes; invert onto wire rack to cool completely.

4. Drizzle melted chocolate over cooled cake, if desired.

Makes 12 servings

ACKNOWLEDGMENTS

**The publisher would like to thank the companies
and organizations listed below for the use of
their recipes and photographs in this publication.**

Campbell Soup Company

Del Monte Foods

The Golden Grain Company®

Nestlé USA

Ortega®, A Division of B&G Foods North America, Inc.

Reckitt Benckiser LLC.

Unilever

A

Almonds
Blackberry Almond Cake, 242
Caribbean Sweet Potato
and Bean Stew, 190
America's Garden Soup, 58
Apples
Apple Peach Dump Cake, 208
Apple Pie Dump Cake, 269
Autumn Dump Cake, 276
Caramel Apple Peanut Cake,
270
Cranberry Apple Cake, 254
Slow-Cooked Autumn Brisket,
184
Sweet-Hot Apple Dump Cake,
264
Apricot Double Chip Cake, 232
Asian Beef and Vegetables, 120
Asian Chicken Noodle Soup, 20
Asian Vegetables and Ham, 164
Asparagus
Creamy Shrimp and Vegetable
Casserole, 138
Ham Asparagus Gratin, 122
Autumn Dump Cake, 276

B

Bacon
Baked Potato Soup, 76
Garlic Potato Soup, 64
Italian Tomato and Pasta Soup,
66
Picante Black Bean Soup, 86
Tuscan Bean & Chicken Soup,
6
Baked Halibut Casserole, 134
Baked Potato Soup, 76
Bananas
Banana Split Cake, 206
Banana Strawberry Dump
Cake, 241
Carrot Banana Cake, 274
Double Banana Cake, 252
Beans
Black and White Mexican Bean
Soup, 90
Caribbean Sweet Potato and
Bean Stew, 190

Beans (continued)
Carolina Baked Beans & Pork
Chops, 142
Confetti Chicken Chili, 168
5-Minute Heat-and-Go Soup,
92
Mediterranean Bean and
Sausage Soup, 34
Middle Eastern Chicken Soup,
18
Minestrone Soup, 84
New Orleans Fish Soup, 48
Pasta Fagioli, 94
Picante Black Bean Soup, 86
Quick Italian Bean, Tomato and
Spinach Soup, 88
Sausage Bean Stew, 167
Simple Turkey Chili, 152
Skillet Southwest Chili, 116
Southwestern Turkey Stew,
104
Three-Bean Mole Chili, 178
Tuscan Bean & Chicken Soup,
6
Beans, Green
America's Garden Soup, 58
Caribbean Sweet Potato and
Bean Stew, 190
Hearty Chicken Vegetable Soup,
24
New World Pork Stew, 185
Beef
Beef Bourguignonne, 196
Beef in Wine Sauce, 130
Country Japanese Noodle
Soup, 37
Meatballs in Burgundy Sauce,
186
Mushroom-Beef Stew, 194
Pizza Meatball and Noodle
Soup, 38
Slow-Cooked Autumn Brisket,
184
Super-Easy Beef Burritos, 180
Beef, Ground
Asian Beef and Vegetables,
120
Chili á la Mexico, 160
Picadillo Tacos, 106

Beef, Ground (continued)
Quick and Zesty Vegetable
Soup, 28
Skillet Southwest Chili, 116
Sweet and Sour Beef, 114
Swirly Noodle Taco Skillet,
96
Black and White Mexican Bean
Soup, 90
Blackberry Almond Cake, 242
Black Forest Cake, 240
Blueberries
Blueberry Cinnamon Cake,
224
Lemon Blueberry Cake, 244
Bow Tie Pasta Bowl, 158

C
Caramel
Autumn Dump Cake, 276
Caramel Apple Peanut Cake,
270
Caramel Candy Cake, 238
Granola Caramel Carrot Cake,
258
Tempting Turtle Cake, 230
Caribbean Sweet Potato and
Bean Stew, 190
Carolina Baked Beans & Pork
Chops, 142
Carrots
America's Garden Soup, 58
Beef Bourguignonne, 196
Carrot Banana Cake, 274
Confetti Chicken Chili, 168
Easy Mushroom Soup, 54
Garlic Potato Soup, 64
Granola Caramel Carrot Cake,
258
Harvest Ham Supper, 180
Hearty Potato and Sausage
Bake, 126
Lentil Soup with Ham, 36
Pizza Meatball and Noodle
Soup, 38
Souped-Up Soup, 63
Thai Noodle Soup, 26
Cha-Cha-Cha Cherry Cake, 220
Cheddar Cheese Soup, 78

Cheesy Tuna Noodle Casserole,
140
Cherries
Banana Split Cake, 206
Black Forest Cake, 240
Cha-Cha-Cha Cherry Cake, 220
Cherry Cheesecake Dump Cake,
228
Rainbow Dump Cake, 248
Chicken
Asian Chicken Noodle Soup, 20
Bow Tie Pasta Bowl, 158
Chicken Couscous, 98
Chicken Florentine in Minutes,
150
Chicken Tortellini Soup, 8
Chunky Chicken Soup, 22
Classic Chicken & Rice, 182
Confetti Chicken Chili, 168
Country Chicken Soup, 14
Creamy Chicken and Rice Bake,
143
Creamy Chicken and Veggie
Soup, 16
Creamy Tortellini with Chicken,
128
Easy Chicken & Biscuits, 132
Easy Chicken Chalupas, 144
Easy Chicken, Spinach and Wild
Rice Soup, 12
Easy Italian Chicken, 176
E-Z Chicken Tortilla Bake, 136
Gumbo in a Hurry, 47
Hearty Chicken Vegetable Soup,
24
Middle Eastern Chicken Soup,
18
Mushroom and Chicken Skillet,
118
Pacific Island Chicken & Rice,
188
Quick Hot and Sour Chicken
Soup, 4
Shrimp and Chicken Paella,
124
Spicy Chicken Chili Mac, 109
Spicy Thai Coconut Soup, 10
Thai Noodle Soup, 26
Tuscan Bean & Chicken Soup, 6

Chili á la Mexico, 160
Chocolate
    Apricot Double Chip Cake, 232
    Banana Split Cake, 206
    Black Forest Cake, 240
    Caramel Candy Cake, 238
    Double Banana Cake, 252
    Pumpkin Chocolate Chip Cake, 278
    Rainbow Dump Cake, 248
    Raspberry Lovers' Dump Cake, 236
    Simple S'More Cake, 204
    Tempting Turtle Cake, 230
Chunky Chicken Soup, 22
Classic Chicken & Rice, 182
Coconut
    Indonesian Curried Soup, 79
    Orange Pineapple Coconut Cake, 214
    Tropical Dump Cake, 222
Confetti Chicken Chili, 168
Corn
    America's Garden Soup, 58
    Black and White Mexican Bean Soup, 90
    Hearty Chicken Vegetable Soup, 24
    New World Pork Stew, 185
    Sausage Bean Stew, 167
    Shrimp & Corn Chowder with Sun-Dried Tomatoes, 50
    Spicy Thai Coconut Soup, 10
Country Chicken Soup, 14
Country Japanese Noodle Soup, 37
Crabmeat
    Gumbo in a Hurry, 47
    Maryland-Style Crab Soup, 46
Cranberries
    Autumn Dump Cake, 276
    Cranberry Apple Cake, 254
    Cranberry Cobbler Cake, 268
    Cranberry Pear Spice Cake, 272
    Orange Cranberry Cake, 262
    Peach Cranberry Upside Down Cake, 250

Creamy Chicken and Rice Bake, 143
Creamy Chicken and Veggie Soup, 16
Creamy Queso Soup, 80
Creamy Shrimp and Vegetable Casserole, 138
Creamy 3-Cheese Pasta, 146
Creamy Tortellini with Chicken, 128
Creamy Tuscan Bean & Chicken Soup, 6
Curried Shrimp and Noodles, 162
Curried Vegetable-Rice Soup, 70

D
Double Banana Cake, 252
Double Pineapple Berry Cake, 202

E
Easy Chicken & Biscuits, 132
Easy Chicken Chalupas, 144
Easy Chicken, Spinach and Wild Rice Soup, 12
Easy Italian Chicken, 176
Easy Mushroom Soup, 54
Easy Skillet Ravioli, 102
E-Z Chicken Tortilla Bake, 136

F
Fish
    Baked Halilbut Casserole, 134
    Cheesy Tuna Noodle Casserole, 140
    Italian Fish Soup, 42
    New Orleans Fish Soup, 48
    Savory Seafood Soup, 44
    Spanish Seafood Stew, 157
5-Minute Heat-and-Go Soup, 92

G
Garlic Potato Soup, 64
Granola Caramel Carrot Cake, 258
Gumbo in a Hurry, 47

H

Ham
 Asian Vegetables and Ham, 164
 Ham Asparagus Gratin, 122
 Harvest Ham Supper, 180
 Lentil Soup with Ham, 36
 Sweet Potato and Ham Soup, 40
Harvest Ham Supper, 180
Hearty Chicken Vegetable Soup, 24
Hearty Potato and Sausage Bake, 126

I

Indonesian Curried Soup, 79
Island Delight Cake, 246
Italian Fish Soup, 42
Italian Sausage and Vegetable Stew, 154
Italian Tomato and Pasta Soup, 66

J

Jerk Turkey Stew, 172

K

Kielbasa & Cabbage Soup, 30

L

Lemon
 Lemon Blueberry Cake, 244
 Pink Lemonade Cake, 215
Lentil Soup with Ham, 36

M

Maryland-Style Crab Soup, 46
Meatballs in Burgundy Sauce, 186
Mediterranean Bean and Sausage Soup, 34
Mexican Casserole with Tortilla Chips, 110
Middle Eastern Chicken Soup, 18
Minestrone Soup, 84
Mixed Berry Dump Cake, 218

Mushrooms
 Beef Bourguignonne, 196
 Beef in Wine Sauce, 130

Mushrooms *(continued)*
 Creamy Shrimp and Vegetable Casserole, 138
 Easy Italian Chicken, 176
 Easy Mushroom Soup, 54
 Italian Sausage and Vegetable Stew, 154
 Mushroom and Chicken Skillet, 118
 Mushroom-Beef Stew, 194
 Spicy Thai Coconut Soup, 10

N

New Orleans Fish Soup, 48
New World Pork Stew, 185
No-Fuss Macaroni and Cheese, 198

O

Orange
 Orange Cranberry Cake, 262
 Orange Pineapple Coconut Cake, 214

P

Pacific Island Chicken & Rice, 188

Pasta & Noodles
 Asian Beef and Vegetables, 120
 Asian Chicken Noodle Soup, 20
 Bow Tie Pasta Bowl, 158
 Cheesy Tuna Noodle Casserole, 140
 Chicken Tortellini Soup, 8
 Country Japanese Noodle Soup, 37
 Creamy 3-Cheese Pasta, 146
 Creamy Tortellini with Chicken, 128
 Curried Shrimp and Noodles, 162
 Easy Skillet Ravioli, 102
 Ham Asparagus Gratin, 122
 Italian Fish Soup, 42
 Italian Tomato and Pasta Soup, 66
 Minestrone Soup, 84

Pasta & Noodles (continued)
No-Fuss Macaroni and Cheese, 198
Pasta Fagioli, 94
Pesto and Tortellini Soup, 60
Pesto Turkey & Pasta, 166
Pizza Meatball and Noodle Soup, 38
Pizza Soup, 62
Quick and Easy Meatball Soup, 32
Quick and Zesty Vegetable Soup, 28
Shrimp Alfredo with Sugar Snap Peas, 170
Shrimp and Pepper Noodle Bowl, 148
Skillet Pasta Roma, 112
Skillet Pesto Tortellini, 108
Souped-Up Soup, 63
Spicy Chicken Chili Mac, 109
Spinach Tortellini Soup, 68
Swirly Noodle Taco Skillet, 96
Szechuan Vegetable Soup, 56
Thai Noodle Soup, 26
Tortellini-Vegetable Toss, 156

Peaches
Apple Peach Dump Cake, 208
Peach Cranberry Upside Down Cake, 250
Peach Melba Dump Cake, 200
Peach Strawberry Cake, 216
Tropical Dump Cake, 222

Pears
Autumn Dump Cake, 276
Cranberry Pear Spice Cake, 272
Triple Ginger Pear Cake, 266

Peas
Cheesy Tuna Noodle Casserole, 140
Easy Mushroom Soup, 54
Pesto and Tortellini Soup, 60
Shrimp Alfredo with Sugar Snap Peas, 170
Shrimp and Chicken Paella, 124
Thai Noodle Soup, 26

Pecans
Apple Pie Dump Cake, 269
Banana Split Cake, 206
Pumpkin Pecan Cake, 256
Tempting Turtle Cake, 230
Tropical Dump Cake, 222
Pesto and Tortellini Soup, 60
Pesto Turkey & Pasta, 166
Picadillo Tacos, 106
Picante Black Bean Soup, 86

Pineapple
Banana Split Cake, 206
Banana Strawberry Dump Cake, 241
Double Pineapple Berry Cake, 202
Granola Caramel Carrot Cake, 258
Island Delight Cake, 246
Orange Pineapple Coconut Cake, 214
Pacific Island Chicken & Rice, 188
Pineapple Angel Cake, 210
Rainbow Dump Cake, 248
Tropical Dump Cake, 222
Pink Lemonade Cake, 215
Pizza Meatball and Noodle Soup, 38
Pizza Soup, 62

Pork
Carolina Baked Beans & Pork Chops, 142
New World Pork Stew, 185
Pork with Mustard and Sauerkraut, 194
Slow Cooker Southwestern Pork Roast, 174

Potatoes
America's Garden Soup, 58
Baked Potato Soup, 76
Creamy Chicken and Veggie Soup, 16
Garlic Potato Soup, 64
Hearty Potato and Sausage Bake, 126
Maryland-Style Crab Soup, 46

Pumpkin
    Pumpkin and Gorgonzola Soup, 82
    Pumpkin Chocolate Chip Cake, 278
    Pumpkin Pecan Cake, 256
    Spicy Pumpkin Soup, 74

Q
Quick and Easy Meatball Soup, 32
Quick and Zesty Vegetable Soup, 28
Quick Hot and Sour Chicken Soup, 4
Quick Italian Bean, Tomato and Spinach Soup, 88

R
Rainbow Dump Cake, 248
Raspberries
    Peach Melba Dump Cake, 200
    Raspberry Lovers' Dump Cake, 236
Red Velvet White Chip Cake, 234
Rice
    Asian Vegetables and Ham, 164
    Classic Chicken & Rice, 182
    Country Chicken Soup, 14
    Creamy Chicken and Rice Bake, 143
    Curried Vegetable-Rice Soup, 70
    Easy Chicken, Spinach and Wild Rice Soup, 12
    Mushroom and Chicken Skillet, 118
    Pacific Island Chicken & Rice, 188
    Shrimp and Chicken Paella, 124
    Spanish Rice with Chorizo, 100

S
Salsa Gazpacho, 52

Sausage
    Hearty Potato and Sausage Bake, 126
    Italian Sausage and Vegetable Stew, 154
    Kielbasa & Cabbage Soup, 30
    Mediterranean Bean and Sausage Soup, 34
    Quick and Easy Meatball Soup, 32
    Sausage Bean Stew, 167
    Skillet Pasta Roma, 112
    Slow Cooker Sausage and Peppers, 192
    Spanish Rice with Chorizo, 100
    Spanish Seafood Stew, 157
Savory Seafood Soup, 44
Shrimp
    Creamy Shrimp and Vegetable Casserole, 138
    Curried Shrimp and Noodles, 162
    Gumbo in a Hurry, 47
    Shrimp Alfredo with Sugar Snap Peas, 170
    Shrimp and Chicken Paella, 124
    Shrimp & Corn Chowder with Sun-Dried Tomatoes, 50
    Shrimp and Pepper Noodle Bowl, 148
Simple S'More Cake, 204
Simple Turkey Chili, 152
Skillet Pasta Roma, 112
Skillet Pesto Tortellini, 108
Skillet Southwest Chili, 116
Slow-Cooked Autumn Brisket, 184
Slow Cooker Sausage and Peppers, 192
Slow Cooker Southwestern Pork Roast, 174
Souped-Up Soup, 63
Southwestern Turkey Stew, 104
Spanish Rice with Chorizo, 100
Spanish Seafood Stew, 157
Spicy Chicken Chili Mac, 109
Spicy Pumpkin Soup, 74

Spicy Thai Coconut Soup, 10
Spinach
  Chicken Florentine in Minutes,
    150
  Chicken Tortellini Soup, 8
  Easy Chicken, Spinach and Wild
    Rice Soup, 12
  Italian Tomato and Pasta Soup,
    66
  Middle Eastern Chicken Soup,
    18
  Pasta Fagioli, 94
  Pesto and Tortellini Soup, 60
  Quick Italian Bean, Tomato
    and Spinach Soup, 88
  Spinach Tortellini Soup, 68
  Sweet Potato and Ham Soup,
    40
  Tuscan Bean & Chicken Soup,
    6
Strawberries
  Banana Strawberry Dump
    Cake, 241
  Peach Strawberry Cake, 216
  Pineapple Angel Cake, 210
  Pink Lemonade Cake, 215
  Super Strawberry Cake, 226
Super-Easy Beef Burritos, 180
Super Fruity Confetti Cake, 212
Super Strawberry Cake, 226
Sweet and Sour Beef, 114
Sweet-Hot Apple Dump Cake,
  264
Sweet Potatoes
  Caribbean Sweet Potato and
    Bean Stew, 190
  Harvest Ham Supper, 180
  Jerk Turkey Stew, 172
  New World Pork Stew, 185
  Slow-Cooked Autumn Brisket,
    184
  Sweet Potato and Ham Soup,
    40
  Sweet Potato Cake, 260
Swirly Noodle Taco Skillet, 96
Szechuan Vegetable Soup, 56

T
Taco Soup, 72

Tempting Turtle Cake, 230
Thai Noodle Soup, 26
Three-Bean Mole Chili, 178
Tortellini-Vegetable Toss, 156
Triple Ginger Pear Cake, 266
Tropical Dump Cake, 222
Turkey
  Jerk Turkey Stew, 172
  Mexican Casserole with Tortilla
    Chips, 110
  Pesto Turkey & Pasta, 166
  Simple Turkey Chili, 152
  Southwestern Turkey Stew,
    104

W
Walnuts
  Carrot Banana Cake, 274
  Cha-Cha-Cha Cherry Cake,
    220
  Cranberry Apple Cake, 254
  Cranberry Pear Spice Cake,
    272
White Chocolate
  Apricot Double Chip Cake,
    232
  Red Velvet White Chip Cake,
    234

Z
Zucchini
  America's Garden Soup, 58
  Chicken Couscous, 98
  Easy Italian Chicken, 176
  Italian Sausage and Vegetable
    Stew, 154
  Pizza Meatball and Noodle
    Soup, 38
  Souped-Up Soup, 63

METRIC
CONVERSION CHART

VOLUME MEASUREMENTS (dry)

$1/8$ teaspoon	= 0.5 mL
$1/4$ teaspoon	= 1 mL
$1/2$ teaspoon	= 2 mL
$3/4$ teaspoon	= 4 mL
1 teaspoon	= 5 mL
1 tablespoon	= 15 mL
2 tablespoons	= 30 mL
$1/4$ cup	= 60 mL
$1/3$ cup	= 75 mL
$1/2$ cup	= 125 mL
$2/3$ cup	= 150 mL
$3/4$ cup	= 175 mL
1 cup	= 250 mL
2 cups = 1 pint	= 500 mL
3 cups	= 750 mL
4 cups = 1 quart	= 1 L

VOLUME MEASUREMENTS (fluid)

1 fluid ounce (2 tablespoons) = 30 mL
4 fluid ounces ($1/2$ cup) = 125 mL
8 fluid ounces (1 cup) = 250 mL
12 fluid ounces ($1 1/2$ cups) = 375 mL
16 fluid ounces (2 cups) = 500 mL

WEIGHTS (mass)

$1/2$ ounce = 15 g
1 ounce = 30 g
3 ounces = 90 g
4 ounces = 120 g
8 ounces = 225 g
10 ounces = 285 g
12 ounces = 360 g
16 ounces = 1 pound = 450 g

DIMENSIONS

$1/16$ inch	= 2 mm
$1/8$ inch	= 3 mm
$1/4$ inch	= 6 mm
$1/2$ inch	= 1.5 cm
$3/4$ inch	= 2 cm
1 inch	= 2.5 cm

OVEN TEMPERATURES

250°F	= 120°C
275°F	= 140°C
300°F	= 150°C
325°F	= 160°C
350°F	= 180°C
375°F	= 190°C
400°F	= 200°C
425°F	= 220°C
450°F	= 230°C

BAKING PAN SIZES

Utensil	Size in Inches/Quarts	Metric Volume	Size in Centimeters
Baking or	$8 \times 8 \times 2$	2 L	$20 \times 20 \times 5$
Cake Pan	$9 \times 9 \times 2$	2.5 L	$23 \times 23 \times 5$
(square or	$12 \times 8 \times 2$	3 L	$30 \times 20 \times 5$
rectangular)	$13 \times 9 \times 2$	3.5 L	$33 \times 23 \times 5$
Loaf Pan	$8 \times 4 \times 3$	1.5 L	$20 \times 10 \times 7$
	$9 \times 5 \times 3$	2 L	$23 \times 13 \times 7$
Round Layer	$8 \times 1 1/2$	1.2 L	20×4
Cake Pan	$9 \times 1 1/2$	1.5 L	23×4
Pie Plate	$8 \times 1 1/4$	750 mL	20×3
	$9 \times 1 1/4$	1 L	23×3
Baking Dish	1 quart	1 L	—
or Casserole	$1 1/2$ quart	1.5 L	—
	2 quart	2 L	—